C000302288

Third edition
Universal Typing

Edith Mackay BA (Hons) FRSA

LEVELS 1 & 2

LONGMAN

Addison Wesley Longman Limited
Edinburgh Gate, Harlow
Essex, CM20 2JE, England
and Associated Companies throughout the world

© Edith Mackay 1979, 1984, 1988

All rights reserved; no part of this publication may be
reproduced, stored in any retrieval system, or transmitted in
any form or by any means, electronic, mechanical,
photocopying, recording, or otherwise without either the prior
written permission of the Publishers or a licence permitting
restricted copying in the United Kingdom issued by the
Copyright Licensing Agency Ltd., 90 Tottenham Court Road,
London W1P 9HE.

*Note. The specimen letterheadings and forms included
in this book may be photocopied for used by students
in carrying out the practice tasks in this book.

This book may not be lent, hired out or otherwise
disposed of by way of trade in any form of binding or cover
other than that in which it is published, without the prior
consent of the Publishers.

First published in Great Britain 1979
Second edition 1984
Third edition 1988
Reprinted 1988, 1990, 1993, 1994, 1996 (twice)
by Addison Wesley Longman Limited
Reprinted 1997

British Library Cataloguing in Publication Data
A catalogue entry for this title is available from the British Library.

ISBN 0 582 30775 9
ISBN Caribbean Edition 0 273 03965 2
© Longman Group UK Limited 1993
Third edition 1993
Reprinted 1994

Library of Congress Cataloging-in-Publication Data
A catalog entry for this title is availabel from the Library of Congress.

Produced by Longman Singapore Publishers Pte Ltd
Printed in Singapore

Foreword

In the future it is probable that a computerised typewriter will be able to produce a usable print-out directly from speech input. But there are still great and complex problems to be solved before that day dawns.

In the meantime our dependence on the typewriter (and in particular the competent operator) increases every year. The growing need for increased output in all areas of communication produces a constant rise in the demand for good typists.

The need for a typing text that embodies the best of modern thinking, yet approaches every topic in the most practical, time-saving and carefully considered way is met by this work of Edith Mackay: it is the best I know, and I am familiar with a great many – from all over the English-speaking world and elsewhere.

I am proud to have played a small part in helping the author, whom I have known for over twenty years, in accomplishing the aims of her project. Its virtues will shine out to student and teacher alike, and it is not for me to extol them here. I would point only to one or two which to me mark this text as different from the rest. Nothing is taken for granted; everything is looked at anew. What is quick, easy to do, and immediately recognisable is taught in preference to other methods. The text is written with an elegance unique in typing texts, yet it is crystal clear and simple enough for all to understand. Few typing books appear that are a pleasure to read. This one is.

Students who follow this course will be more than good typists: they will be thoughtful and concerned operators who will achieve high standards because they have come to understand the need for them.

This book is written with both learning and teaching in mind. Teachers will find that it lifts much of the day-to-day burden from their shoulders, and so enables them to devote more of their time to the vital work of observing individuals and giving them the help, encouragement and guidance that they need.

Bert Canning

Preface

This enlarged and updated edition of Universal Typing is designed to meet the needs of advancing communications technology – which has impacted on all aspects of life. Electronic QWERTY keyboards are now used virtually everywhere as a communication tool, and the ability to operate them efficiently has become little short of a necessity. As a result, keyboarding and typewriting skills are being taught to ever growing numbers of students at school and college, and more and more people are learning on their own.

The three main sections of this book meet three important needs: (1) Development of sound keyboarding skills; (2) Guidance and practice in basic production techniques required for Level 1 examinations and junior employment; and (3) Development of greater competence required for Level 2 examinations and employment at a higher level.

Most students will learn in class with a teacher. However, instructions are sufficiently clear and detailed for students learning on their own.

Main features of the course

After a short introductory section, there are 137 Units of work. New 'theory' is introduced in small steps, each step leading on logically to the next one so that learners feel a real sense of progression and build-up of skill. For ease of reference, all theory is printed on a tinted background, and there is a comprehensive index.

The important skill of **typing from manuscript copy** is started early (in Unit 20) together with the various methods used by writers to amend their draft text.

There is a comprehensive range of **keyboard/technique drills** included in the Units as warm-up practice. In addition, there is an 'Error Clinic' of drills given in Unit 13.

Because it is crucial for learners to develop **accuracy and speed** together, an effective technique for this is incorporated in the text – ranging from one-minute to ten-minute timings (see Units 8 and 138).

The vital importance of **proof-reading** is emphasised throughout the book. It is stressed that 'mailable' or 'usable' standard is the only acceptable one for any completed document in examinations and in office work. When students are encouraged to adopt this high standard in practice work it stands them in good stead in examinations and in employment.

Continuous text skills – applicable to the full range of business documents – are conveniently grouped together after keyboard learning, and used in all the subsequently introduced documents.

Each topic (letters, memos, tabulation, etc) is dealt with as a whole in a group of consecutive Units. The two Contents pages show the full coverage at Levels 1 and 2. The consolidation production task Units ensure that completed topics are systematically kept in practice. To add realism to the work, printed letterheads, memo-heads, etc, are included for the students to cut out, photocopy, and use in their practice tasks.

At the end of Level 1 training, examination requirements at that level are summarised and followed by a Mock Level 1 examination. The same procedure is repeated at the end of the Level 2 work.

Word processing assignments (10) are included at Level 2 to help students develop self-reliance at the word processor.

The following **companion books** are available·
1. Universal Typing Student Key and Notes, Levels 1 and 2
2. Universal Typing Realistic Office Assignments, Level 1
3. Universal Typing Realistic Office Assignments, Level 2

Acknowledgements

This new edition reflects various helpful and constructive suggestions made to the publishers and author by both teachers and students. Such comments are always welcome and carefully considered when a new edition is prepared. My thanks go to Margaret Berriman and Howard Bailey of Pitman for helping to make this new edition forward looking and attractive to look at and use.

EM

Contents
(Keyboarding and Level 1)

Contents
(Level 2)

Index

	Words	Strokes
If a man is posted to work abroad, he will probably expect living	13	66
conditions and local customs to be vastly different from what they	27	133
are at home. But if he is sent to work, abroad, in the same company	41	203
as the one he works for at home, he is likely to expect to find few	54	271
differences there. He will tend to assume that the company is an	68	338
island of stability in a sea of change. Of course, certain national	82	408
traits will show: the Germans will work harder, the French will be	96	478
more explosive, and the Italians more easy-going; but it will	108	541
basically be the same old company doing the same old things in	121	604
the same old way.	124	622
This seems to be far from the truth. It seems, in fact, that	137	687
the difference in working methods and relationships is a greater	150	752
source of friction and misunderstanding than anything else. For	164	818
instance, a German was posted to work at the head of an important	177	885
technical section of his firm's City of London branch. He was	190	951
a stickler for an early start in the morning, but he found he	203	1013
could not goad his senior colleagues into coming into the office	216	1078
before ten in the morning, nor could he break them of their	228	1138
two-hour lunch habits.	232	1161
It was several weeks before he found out that his minions made	245	1226
a habit of working in the office until eight or nine at night –	258	1290
long after he had gone home - clearing up details that he usually	271	1356
dealt with early in the morning. Since a good deal of the	283	1416
branch's business was with America, he decided that the British	297	1483
methods were more effective than his own, and he changed his	309	1544
own working hours, much to the annoyance of his wife.	320	1598
The other side of the picture shows that British and American	333	1664
managers in West Germany often complain that although the local	346	1730
staff are hard-working, they are rigid in their approach to	358	1790
working hours and to the work itself. Staff may come in at	370	1851
seven in the morning, and keep strictly to lunch and coffee	382	1911
breaks, but they are off like a shot at three in the afternoon,	395	1975
whatever the work load.	400	1999

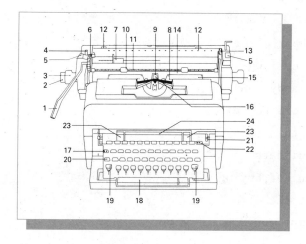

Manual typebar machine

Single element machine

There are differences from make to make and from model to model. Use your machine booklet if necessary to find the parts on *your* machine, and to check how they work.

1	Carriage return lever or key	10	Paper grips	19	Shift keys
2	Variable line spacer	11	Paper bail scale	20	Shift lock
3	Cylinder knobs	12	Margin stops	21	Colour change adjuster
4	Interliner	13	Paper-release lever	22	Back-space key
5	Carriage release levers	14	Platen roller (cylinder)	23	Tabulator set and clear key
6	Line-space selector	15	Transparent paper holders	24	Tabulator bar/key
7	Paper guide	16	Printing point indicator	25	Print carrier
8	Alignment scale	17	Margin release key	26	Printing element
9	Card holder	18	Space bar	27	Half-space correction key

2 **Variable line spacer** This knob, at the end of the left cylinder knob, is operated to enable matter to be typed above or below the typing line. It must then be used to adjust back to the normal typing line.

3 **Cylinder knobs** (one either side) move the paper up or down.

6 **Line-space selector** regulates the depth of space between lines of type.

7 **Paper guide** against which the left edge of the paper is positioned as it is inserted in the machine.

11 **Paper bail scale** – the movable arm, marked with a paper scale, on which the paper grips are mounted.

Paper scales help the planning of work across the page. They are situated on the paper bail scale (11) on the alignment scale (8) and sometimes across the front of the machine (shown in the single element machine diagram).

13 **Paper release lever** – when pulled forward releases pressure on the paper for straightening it,

etc. Should be used when moving paper from the machine.

15 **Transparent paper holders** These pieces of plastic, positioned either side of the printing point, have three uses: (*a*) they include an alignment scale, which indicates the base of the type; (*b*) they hold small papers, cards, or envelopes in position for typing; (*c*) they enable ruling to be carried out. (The two holes in the plastic – one either side of the printing point – are for the insertion of a pencil, ball-point pen or a stylus in stencil work.)

17 **Margin release key** when depressed allows typing beyond the margin stops at either end of the line.

23 **Tabulator set/clear keys** are used for column work, indented paragraphs, etc. Used in conjunction with the tab bar or key, the machine moves speedily to the tab stop positions in turn. Always clear all previous settings when starting a fresh piece of work.

25 **Print carrier** (single element machines) moves across the page instead of the carriage moving as on typebar machines.

SI 1.40

	Words	Strokes

On the advice of a salesman, a friend of mine prepared for — 12 / 59

the visit of a prospective buyer of her house by curling — 23 / 116

up with a calf-bound book, a glass of Napoleon brandy, and — 35 / 176

her video flickering in an alcove. The strategy was to sell — 48 / 238

not just a house, but an image of affluence. In this case — 60 / 298

it did not succeed, but it is a principle that builders — 71 / 354

apply with their show-houses. If you are thinking of buying — 83 / 416

a house on a new estate, be on your guard against the — 94 / 470

seductive comforts set up by professionals to tempt you. — 105 / 527

Before entering a show-house, take a walk through the — 117 / 583

development to get an impression of what the site will look — 129 / 643

like when it is finished. If the site looks tidy and — 140 / 698

organized, the rest of the project will probably be well- — 151 / 756

managed too. The brickwork of the show-house should be even, — 164 / 819

clean and free from mortar chippings; the seals round the — 175 / 877

windows should be intact; and the exterior paintwork even. — 187 / 936

Look closely at the roof. Are the tiles sound and evenly laid? — 201 / 1003

Are the flashings round dormer windows and chimneys well — 212 / 1061

trimmed? Test windows and doors to see if they open smoothly — 225 / 1125

and are not liable to scrape and rattle or create a draught. — 237 / 1186

In the kitchen pay particular attention to the units. Are they — 251 / 1253

sturdy and securely fitted? Check the depth of the work — 262 / 1312

surfaces and be sure they match your domestic appliances. Make — 275 / 1377

sure the plumbing is tidy, and that extra water supplies for — 288 / 1438

items such as a dishwasher can be fitted. Note the extent of — 300 / 1501

built-in storage space and fitted wardrobes, as these can be of — 313 / 1565

great value in terms of cost and convenience. Look out for — 325 / 1626

insulation extras which help to keep down fuel bills. — 336 / 1680

When you leave the show-house, look inside a similar empty — 348 / 1740

house. It will give you a different perspective on the space — 361 / 1803

available, and a second chance to check the standards of — 372 / 1860

workmanship. You may be more critical of finish in a house — 384 / 1921

where you are not distracted by pretty curtains, deep-pile — 396 / 1980

carpets – and that alluring atmosphere that the builder has — 408 / 2040

tried to create. — 411 / 2057

Electronic typewriter keyboard

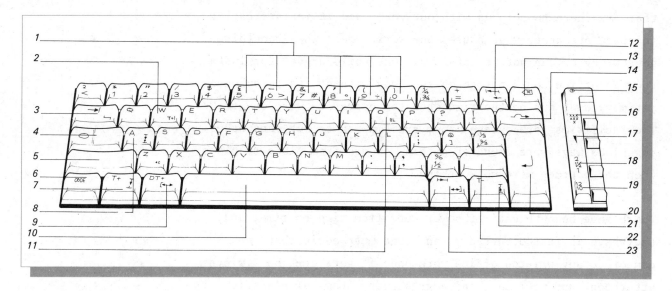

Summary of keyboard operating controls

1 Keys with 6 additional symbols for the 100 character typewheel
2 Tabulator key with vertical line
3 Tabular key and automatic paragraph indentation
4 Shift lock key with indicator lamp
5 Left-hand shift key
6 CODE key
7 Tab set key and paper transport upwards (also half-line spacing)
8 Automatic paper insertion/ejection key
9 Decimal tab key and left margin key
10 Space bar
11 ON-LINE key used with interface box to computer connection for using the typewriter as a printer

12 Backspace and printer return without line spacing key and left margin release key
13 Correction key
14 Relocate key and right margin release key
15 ON control lamp
16 Switch for expand, bold print and normal print
17 Impression control
18 Line spacing switch 1-, 1½- and 2-line
19 Pitch selector for 10 and 12 pitch
20 Printer return with line spacing
21 Tab clear key and paper transport downwards. (also half-line spacing)
22 Right-hand shift key
23 Half-space key and key to set right-hand margin

All keys have a repeat function when held down.

Some electronic typewriter keyboards are more sophisticated than the one shown above, others less so. Also, there are considerable differences from make to make and from model to model. Procedures for using the various functions vary from machine to machine, so check your instruction manual. Some capabilities of electronic typewriters are given below.

- Corrections are simple. A window display panel enables the typist to detect and correct errors in the text *before* it is committed to paper or memory.

- Memory will automatically print out date, signature block, short texts, etc, as well as reproduce page formats. Where machines have a sufficiently large memory it is possible to mail merge, eg a list of names and addresses within a circular letter.

- Operator prompts, eg to show the remaining amount of memory, or when an instruction to the machine is not given properly.

- Ribbon changes are quick and clean with the cassette system.
- Ruling facility for horizontal and vertical lines.
- Scientific, mathematical, and foreign language text is undertaken by use of the appropriate daisy wheel or (with IBM machines) golf ball print element.
- Search operation. In edit mode a symbol, word, phrase or other character string can be set for search (for amendment, etc).
- Typeface and pitch changeover is simple by use of different daisy wheels.

Sophisticated electronic typewriters have many features in common with word processors. The two most important differences between them are:

a Greater storage capability of word processors.
b Word processors have a TV-like screen as distinct from an electronic typewriter's narrow window display panel.

	Words	Strokes
	SI 1.37	

In an office we depend a great deal on the aids and machines | 12 | 62
that are there to help us with our work, and it is interesting | 25 | 125
to speculate about what causes the worst chaos when something | 37 | 187
goes wrong or can not be obtained. One could argue, for instance, | 51 | 255
that an office could not go on for long without its telephones: | 64 | 320
yet many did, during the time when the operators were on strike. | 77 | 385
The facilities for postage, too, are important; but many other | 90 | 449
ingenious ways were found of getting papers from place to place | 103 | 513
when the postmen were not working. | 110 | 548

There have been threats of power cuts from time to time, and | 122 | 611
they have in fact occurred often. One must admit that one | 134 | 671
cannot do any written office work once it gets dark on a winter | 147 | 735
afternoon, during a cut; and a great many items of electric | 159 | 795
machinery at once become quite useless for the time being. | 171 | 854
(The manual typewriter may have a longer future than we think.) | 184 | 920
The number of cups of tea and coffee that can be drunk goes | 196 | 981
down; and some unlucky workers may find themselves stuck in the | 209 | 1045
lift until such time as the power comes on again. | 219 | 1095

When paper is in short supply there are apt to be difficulties; | 232 | 1161
though at the same time it is clear that economy in the use of | 245 | 1224
existing paper stocks is one of the easiest things to achieve | 257 | 1286
in times of shortage – provided of course that the telephone | 269 | 1347
is still working. | 273 | 1365

It seems that at the present time the thing that has the most | 286 | 1429
crippling effect in the office is the sudden lack of the | 297 | 1486
photocopier, when it is out of commission. The whole tempo of | 310 | 1550
work has to change to meet this new situation: time has to be | 323 | 1613
made for taking carbon copies; for reading matter over the | 334 | 1672
phone; for taking a document round from one person to | 345 | 1726
another, or getting people to come and look at it, instead | 357 | 1785
of just sending them a copy of it. A meeting where everything | 370 | 1849
has to be explained orally becomes much longer than one where | 382 | 1911
papers have been read in advance, even if they have had to be | 395 | 1973
read at quite short notice. | 400 | 2001

Paper	The most common size is A4 (210 mm × 297 mm; approximately 8¼″ × 11¾″). Start by using only this size, with the shorter side at the top.
Size of type	The three most common sizes are **pica** (or 10-pitch), **elite** (or 12-pitch) and **micro** (or 15-pitch). Examples follow.

Pica type has 10 characters to the inch (2.5 cm).

Elite type has 12 characters to the inch (2.5 cm).

Micro type has 15 characters to the inch (2.5 cm).

Many modern machines can use micro type, but for learning it is best to use pica or elite. They are larger and easier to proofread.

Setting margins

Typewriters have two margin controls – one for the left, the other for the right. Look in your instruction booklet if there is no-one to show you how to set them.

The left setting you will first use is pica 25 or elite 35 (with the left edge of the paper at 0 on the paper scales). To begin with you will not use the right-hand margin setting as you will follow the copy line by line. (Machines with automatic line turn-up should be used in normal typewriter mode at the early learning stage.)

Line space selector

This has a 1 2 3 scale, sometimes with in-between settings as well (1½ 2½). It regulates the space between the lines of type, as shown below.

	Line space selector at 1	*Line space selector at 2*	*Line space selector at 3*
2.5 cm **(1 in)** **6 lines**	This is typed in single line spacing. There is no full line of space between the lines of type. But the lines are, of course, clearly separated.	In double spacing there *(space)* is one full line of *(space)* space between the type.	In treble spacing 2 *(space)* *(space)* lines of space are *(space)* *(space)* left between the type.

Position at machine

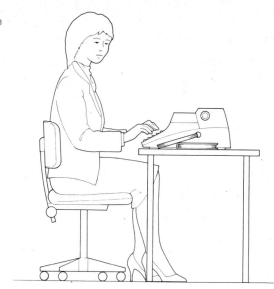

Posture Checklist
1 Eyes on copy.
2 Back supported by chair.
3 Book sloping to prevent eye-strain.
4 Feet flat on floor.

Always adjust the height and position of your chair so you do not have to stretch the arms or crouch.

The aim is to achieve a comfortable position which will avoid fatigue and assist your work.

	SI 1.40	Words	Strokes

The laser beam is a space-age supertool - the magic torch with a host of diverse functions. Nowhere is its potential more far-reaching than in the field of medicine, where it has streamlined surgery and inspired new treatments for many ills. But how does it work? Unlike ordinary light, which is made up of different wavelengths that shift at random, laser light is composed of just one frequency. Its light waves are aligned in tight parallel lines which move as a single pulse in one direction only. That is why an 8-watt argon laser is able to produce energy a thousand times as strong as the sun, its beam so minutely focused that it can pinpoint a single blood cell and punch seven holes in it.

Words		Strokes
13		65
26		129
39		194
53		263
66		331
79		397
92		462
106		528
119		593
131		656
143		714

Since laser light must first be absorbed, its use in medicine is largely dictated by wavelength. For instance, the blue-green beam of the argon laser will pass straight through tissue that has no pigment, and be absorbed by the red blood cells. So it is ideal for treating tumours, bleaching birthmarks or punching a hole in the iris of a person with glaucoma. The stronger infra-red laser will stem deep-seated bleeding and break up kidney stones, or kill some cancers; but since its beam is not visible, it must first be mounted on an 'aiming beam' to spotlight its target.

Words		Strokes
156		781
170		849
183		914
196		980
209		1045
222		1112
236		1179
249		1245
260		1300

The carbon dioxide 'laser knife' has an invisible beam too, but its frequency is absorbed by all tissues. It can replace a scalpel. A laser knife can cut and seal off human tissue in a fraction of the time and trauma involved in traditional surgery. There is no risk of infection as the laser sterilises the tissues and does not need a general anaesthetic. Since there is no incision, stitches and scars could well become a thing of the past. And the laser is so accurate that only the affected points are treated: there is no risk to the healthy surrounding parts.

Words		Strokes
274		1372
288		1442
302		1509
315		1577
329		1644
342		1710
355		1777
368		1842
376		1881

Plastic surgeons and ear, nose and throat specialists have welcomed the laser. The one-time fiddly business of removing lumps, bumps, blemishes and growths becomes simple in the hands of the experts. Since treatment takes just a few minutes, many more patients can be treated in the same time than by former methods.

Words		Strokes
390		1951
404		2019
417		2085
431		2154
441		2203

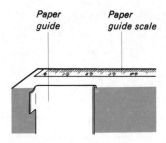

Paper guide   Paper guide scale

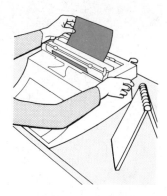

Line space selector set at 1 for single spacing.

Paper guide Make sure this is lined up with 0 on the paper scales.

Insert A4 paper using a backing sheet or second sheet of paper. The method of inserting paper varies with different machines. On *electronic typewriters* there may be a paper insertion lever, or you may need to press the Code key together with the Paper Insertion key. Consult your machine booklet. With *manual typewriters*, hold the double paper in your left hand, backing sheet towards you. Slip it between the roller and paper rest with the left edge of the paper against the paper guide (positioned at 0). Turn the right-hand knob to draw the paper up round the roller.

Straighten paper if necessary, using the paper release lever.

Top of paper Adjust the paper so you will start typing approximately one inch from the top.

Set left margin
Left: Pica 25, Elite 35
(Move right margin control to the extreme right position – out of the way – for the present.)

Position at machine Check your position against the Posture Checklist on page 3.

You can now begin to type.

Practical tip Rule two thick black lines on your backing sheet 38 mm and 25 mm from the bottom. They will show through the typing paper and ensure you leave 25 mm blank space at the foot of the page.

There are still many people who dislike central heating in | 12 | 59
the home, and who believe that both on health and cost grounds | 24 | 122
the old system of coal, electric or gas fires in separate rooms | 37 | 186
is to be preferred. Even so, the hardiest fresh air fiends | 49 | 247
will readily admit that their fuel bills these days are a big | 62 | 309
item in the household budget. Every form of fuel costs more | 74 | 371
and more each year. Heating the home in winter is now a | 86 | 429
financial burden to many people, especially the old and the | 98 | 489
sick. Yet the bills can be reduced both quickly and simply | 110 | 550
without any reduction in the standard of living, whatever form | 123 | 613
of heating is used. | 127 | 633

Those tiny little gaps in window frames and larger ones around | 140 | 698
doors let in draughts equivalent to a hole in the wall as big | 152 | 760
as four square feet. The loss could be as much as thirty per | 165 | 823
cent of the heat costs for a family in an average three-bedroomed | 178 | 889
house. It would pay handsomely to spend money sealing up all | 190 | 952
those cracks! The old-fashioned 'dog' or 'sausage' along the | 204 | 1022
bottom of the door is the cheapest way to help exclude the cold | 217 | 1086
draughts - this can be simply a sewn-up roll of heavy cloth, | 229 | 1147
easy to lay down and pick up when necessary. A brush-style door | 243 | 1213
flap or a plastic flap is very inexpensive. For draughty windows | 256 | 1280
there are available cheap sealants, foam strips, and copper or | 269 | 1343
bronze strips. Full heavy curtains are very good insulators, and | 282 | 1410
when drawn can be as effective as double glazing. But you should | 295 | 1477
close them as soon as the sun goes down. If left open, the room | 309 | 1543
temperature can drop by an extra five degrees overnight. | 320 | 1600

A further effective way to reduce heat waste is to fit a jacket | 333 | 1666
to the hot water cylinder: it will pay for itself in under a year. | 347 | 1734
Above all with central heating, you should ask yourself whether | 360 | 1799
you are overheating your rooms. By turning down the thermostat | 373 | 1864
one or two degrees, you can knock five per cent off the bill. | 385 | 1926
Upstairs, electric blankets, hot water bottles, or just more | 398 | 1988
blankets on the beds work out much cheaper than leaving the | 410 | 2048
central heating on in the bedrooms - and are enough for most | 422 | 2109
people except when it is very cold. The old-fashioned solution to | 435 | 2177
cold weather - wearing a warm sweater - should not be forgotten. | 448 | 2242

Typewriter operation

Fingers over home keys

Place your fingers just above the home keys (in colour on the above diagram) with G and H 'free' in the middle. This is the position from which all other keys are located in 'touch typing'.

Striking the keys

Electronic and electric machines Activate each key with a light 'touch'.

Manuals Strike each key firmly and sharply.

Practise striking the home keys in any order – to get the right action and 'feel'. Then type the following line of home row letters. Use the above diagram and keep your eyes on the book as much as possible. Say each letter to yourself as you type it.

`ffffaaaajjjj;;;;ffffaaaajjjj;;;;`   *Turn up for new line*

Starting new lines

Electronics and electrics Quickly strike the Return key with the little finger of the right hand. (In Automatic mode, electronic typewriters automatically start new lines when the right-hand margin is set. For the present, use Normal typewriter mode with the right-hand margin at the extreme right position.)

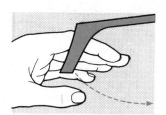

Manuals The carriage return lever is operated by a quick sweep of the left hand and forearm. The hand should be held flat (with the palm down and fingers closed) and should strike the lever with just enough force to ensure that the carriage reaches the left margin stop. The left hand should move quickly back to its home keys: the right hand does not move from its home keys.

You should soon be able to start new lines without looking up. Always turn up for a new line *immediately* after striking the last letter of the line.

Many typists think in terms of their 'speed'. This often shows   *14*   *68*
a keen attitude to their work, but it is important to know just   *26*   *132*
what is meant.   *30*   *148*

In the first place, any valid claim to speed must assume a   *42*   *208*
satisfactory accuracy with it. As has been emphasized   *53*   *264*
throughout this book, the one is useless without the other.   *65*   *324*
This apart, many factors have to be considered. A very short   *78*   *388*
burst of speed might be achieved which could not be maintained   *90*   *451*
over a long period. A passage made up of short sentences with   *103*   *515*
plain words and simple syntax can always be typed more rapidly   *116*   *578*
than a complex one in unfamiliar language. If the typist has   *128*   *641*
to pause over difficult words and syntax, then speed must   *140*   *699*
suffer. If therefore the copy is too easy, the typist gets a   *152*   *762*
false impression of her speed; if it is too difficult, she   *164*   *821*
cannot do justice to herself.   *170*   *852*

Examinations take account of these problems. They aim to test   *183*   *917*
all candidates on standard copy so that there is a common   *195*   *975*
measurement of speed - with of course the same treatment of   *207*   *1035*
errors. (Alas, they cannot cope with the fact that in typing   *220*   *1099*
we all have off days when the mind and the fingers just will   *232*   *1159*
not work!)   *235*   *1174*

Employers like to have a national speed qualification as   *246*   *1232*
evidence of training and ability. They know that no tests can   *259*   *1296*
adequately reflect the work in an office. This must be learned   *272*   *1361*
on the job. The point is that with the foundation of a fast   *285*   *1423*
and accurate typing speed, the typist can devote her mind more   *297*   *1486*
fully to the problems of the office production tasks - and do   *310*   *1548*
these faster too.   *313*   *1565*

Now type these two lines several times:

```
ddddaaaakkkk;;;;ddddaaaakkkk;;;;
ssssaaaallll;;;;ssssaaaallll;;;;
```

Return for new line
Return twice to leave one line of space

Using the space bar

The space bar should be tapped sharply with the thumb. (Most people prefer to use the right-hand thumb, but if you are left-handed you may find using the left thumb easier. Whichever you adopt, *it is best always to use the same thumb*.)

Each time you tap the space bar, one space will appear on the paper. Keep your fingers over the home keys while you operate it.

Now type this line three times as shown, with one space after each letter. Say each letter to yourself as you type it. And say *space* to yourself each time you tap the space bar.

```
a ; s l d k f j a ; s l d k f j
a ; s l d k f j a ; s l d k f j
a ; s l d k f j a ; s l d k f j
```

Did you remember to:

1 keep your fingers over the home keys?
2 strike the keys correctly?
3 concentrate and say each letter to yourself as you typed it?
4 say *space* each time you tapped the space bar?
5 leave one space after each character?
6 keep your eyes on the book as much as possible?

If all your answers are *yes*, you will start Unit 1 with confidence. If your answer is no to any of the questions, copy the above line of typing again in the correct manner.

Division of alphanumeric keyboard into hand and fingering units for 'touch' typing

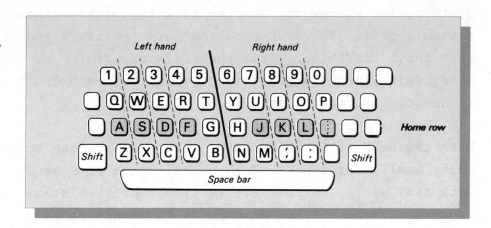

	Words	Strokes
People of all ages in all parts of the world have always loved	13	64
gardens. This was as true of the Greeks and Romans, and other	26	130
ancient civilizations, as it is of every country in the modern	39	193
world. Gardening can bring the wonders and beauty of nature	51	255
to the homes of everyone. Whether in a large or small garden,	64	319
on a terrace or balcony, or just in a few indoor plant pots,	76	380
the pleasure of growing things is the same. As part of our	88	441
daily lives we can all enjoy the cycle of nature from the tiny	101	504
seed to the full-blown flower, yielding its own new seed to	113	564
start the process all over again.	120	599

	Words	Strokes
Indoor gardening is an art in itself. There are flowering	132	660
house plants and decorative foliage plants for all rooms. As	145	723
with any living thing, plants need moisture, food and light.	157	784
Also of course, for good health, these should be in the right	169	847
amounts. With a little patience and skill, the results can be	182	911
delightful. Merely growing things, however, has an exciting	195	973
charm of its own.	198	990

Passage 9   *SI 1.38*

	Words	Strokes
Stamp collecting is a hobby which gives equal interest and	12	60
pleasure from youth to old age. For a start, you have	23	116
portraits and pictures in a wealth of colour, delightful to	35	176
the eye. Then, as you acquire the stamps of different	46	232
countries, your knowledge of geography grows - and no less of	59	294
history, for stamps are used to mark the great events in a	71	353
nation's past. The best-known authors, painters and composers	83	417
have their place too. From the realm of nature you will find	96	480
bird, animal and floral stamps, typical of each country.	107	537
Technology is covered as well.	114	569

	Words	Strokes
With the help of an illustrated catalogue you can build up at	126	632
quite small cost a wide-ranging collection of stamps dating	138	692
back many years in time. It is true that rare stamps are	150	751
expensive, some costing as much as thousands of pounds. There	163	815
is, however, a wealth of choice between the cheapest and	174	872
dearest stamps. Anyone who puts money into a collection has	187	934
the knowledge that over the years stamps have proved to be a	199	995
good investment.	202	1011

Paper A4 size with left edge at 0 on paper scales.

Margins (for Units 1–7) Left: pica 20, elite 30
Right: move to extreme right position, out of the way.

Copy each line at least twice. Use single spacing (selector at 1) but leave one line of space before moving to a new line of copy (by using return twice).

Mistakes should be ignored at this stage. *Concentrate on developing the correct finger movements.*

Proofreading At regular intervals, carefully check your typescript *letter for letter* and *space for space* against the book. Draw a ring round each word or group of letters that contains one or more errors. Count the ringed words and write the number in a circle in the margin opposite the last line checked. If any letter is repeatedly wrong, give it special attention.

Use thumb for space bar. Say each letter as you type it and 'think' the finger you are using.

Practise home keys	**1**	asdf ;lkj asdf ;lkj asdf ;lkj asdf ;lkj;
	2	ass add aff ;ll ;kk ;jj ass add aff ;ll;
	3	fdd fss faa jkk jll j;; fdd fss faa jkkj
	4	aff ;jj add ;kk ass ;ll aff ;jj add ;kk;
	5	faa j;; fss jll fdd jkk faa j;; fss jllj
Word building	**6**	a as ass lass alas alaska ask asks flask
	7	a all fall falls a add dad lads fad fads
Use home keys *(one space after ;)*	**8**	a jaffa salad; alaska salad; all salads;
	9	a lass falls; lads fall; dad falls alas;
	10	ask a lad; ask a lass; ask dad; ask all;

UNIT 1   Home keys

	Words	Strokes
It sometimes happens that an angry person storms into a	11	57
typist's office waving a sheet of paper and demanding to know	24	120
why anyone ever typed this. He points out that it makes no	36	181
sense and insists that he could never have written such	47	237
rubbish.	49	247

What has happened is a common pitfall when typing from copy.	62	309
The typist, not thinking about the sense of what she is typing,	75	374
and not keeping her eyes on the copy as much as she should, has	88	438
missed out whole lines. This is a common error, particularly	100	501
when the same word is repeated on the next line or a little	112	561
further down. The word is picked up in the wrong place - and	125	624
typed nonsense results.	130	649

Of course, such an angry situation would not arise if the typed	143	714
work was carefully checked before being passed as finished.	155	774
One has to be particularly alert when typing speed tests - as	167	837
this kind of mistake is more common than you may think.	178	892

It is easy to see why jogging is popular. We all know that	12	62
regular exercise in the fresh air plays a big part in keeping	25	124
a fit and healthy body. Yet many of us have no aptitude or	37	185
liking for games, nor have we any chance to play them	48	239
regularly. The same applies to many other pastimes - like	60	299
swimming, gymnastics, skating or dancing - and they are not,	72	360
of course, always possible in the open air.	81	404

The merit of jogging is that it can be done where people	92	462
please, at any hour of the day or night, by persons of any	104	521
age, either alone or in company. A round of the city or	116	579
suburban house blocks is as good as a cross-country run. The	128	642
jogger can set his or her own pace, and if necessary drop the	141	704
trot to a walk till breath is recovered.	149	746

While the natural loner enjoys jogging alone, many people	161	805
prefer to go out with friends in groups of joggers formed in	173	866
offices and neighbourhoods. The choice is entirely their own.	186	928

Technique points

Sitting position at machine is important to prevent eye-strain, aches and pains – often the cause of errors. Revise the checklist on page 3.

Hands Keep fingers over the home keys, moving away only to strike another key.

Key striking should be brisk.

Eyes on the book (the copy) as much as possible. As you type, say each letter to yourself and 'think' the finger you are using.

Each new key *a* Practise finger movement from home key and back *looking* at the keyboard.
b Then *without looking* till really confident of the movement.
c Start typing new key from the book.
Follow this procedure for every new key as you come to it.

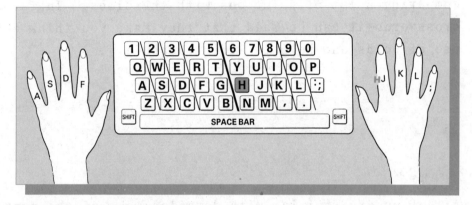

Re-read instructions at the top of Unit 1.
Warm-up practice *Start each Unit by practising one or two lines from the bottom of the previous Unit.*

H
Use J finger

1 jjh jjh jjh jhh jhh jhh jhj jhj jhj jhhj
2 a; as; has; a all hall; hall hall shall;
3 a; add; had; as has; has had; hall shall

Word building

4 a as has ash dash lash flash sash slash;
5 as all hall halls lash shall had salads;

6 a lass has salad; a lad has had a salad;
7 a lad shall fall; a lass has had a fall;

Revise all keys learned

8 dad has flasks; lads fall as flak falls;
9 dad has fads'; ash falls; dad shall lash;
10 a lass had a jaffa salad; all had salad;
11 a lad shall ask a lass; dad has a flask;
12 a lass has a sash; lads had jaffa salad;

People seem to like or dislike crossword puzzles - with quite   *13*   *63*
strong feeling. The crossword lover can scarcely glance at   *25*   *124*
the news headlines before having a shot at the puzzle. To   *37*   *184*
those who do not have such interest, the chequer-board which   *49*   *245*
appears each day on its allotted page is something to be   *60*   *302*
totally ignored.   *64*   *320*

No doubt a liking for crosswords depends to some extent on a   *76*   *381*
measure of success in solving them. This may take some time,   *89*   *444*
as there are conventions and verbal quirks in the setting of   *101*   *505*
crosswords that can only be recognized with practice and by   *113*   *565*
comparing a lot of solutions with the clues. In favour of   *125*   *625*
crosswords it can be said that they make you think about the   *137*   *686*
use of words and help to widen vocabulary.   *146*   *728*

All of us are familiar with detailed maps of the continents   *12*   *61*
and land masses of the world. We are also aware that maps   *14*   *121*
have been made of the Moon and, more recently, of Mars. It   *37*   *184*
therefore perhaps comes as a surprise to realise that, apart   *49*   *245*
from a few small areas, no detailed maps of the ocean floor   *61*   *305*
exist; knowledge is scanty even of the more shallow   *71*   *357*
continental shelves.   *76*   *379*

Cameras cannot be used for sea-floor mapping because of the   *88*   *440*
lack of light. Thus it is necessary to use techniques that   *100*   *501*
make use of sound waves. A way of scanning the sea bed by   *112*   *561*
means of a narrow sound beam has been successfully used on   *124*   *620*
the deep ocean beds as well as on the easier continental   *135*   *677*
shelves. In this way a picture of the contours can be   *147*   *733*
gradually built up. It is, however, a slow process, and it   *159*   *794*
will be some years before such a mammoth task is completed.   *171*   *853*

Don't forget warm-up practice. Re-read instructions and hints at top of Units 1 and 2.

E
Use D finger

1   dde dde dde dee dee dee ded ded ded deed

2   deed heed ell fell; eel heel ease easel;

3   dales kale sales; jade jaded fade faded;

4   he fell dead; she fell dead; heads fell;

5   he feels sad; she sells eels; she leads;

G
Use F finger

6   ffg ffg ffg fgg fgg fgg fgf fgf fgf fggf

7   fag lag sag jag; edge ledge sedge hedge;

8   a as gas; gaff gall gale; egg legs kegs;

9   a glad lass had eggs; she sells glasses;

10   a gas leak flashed; he has jagged a leg;

N
Use J finger

11   jjn jjn jjn jnn jnn jnn jnj jnj jnj jnnj

12   jeans sane lane need nag send lend fend;

13   ankle knee keen seen hen den lens sense;

14   he needs gas leads; he kneels; send ale;

15   lend dad a hand; send hen feed and sand;

Revise all keys learned

16   she sells jade and shells; he sells ale;

17   gales lash seas; hedges and lakes flash;

18   a sad lad has a keen head and lean hand;

19   she has a faded jade fan and glass eggs;

20   a lass and lad held hands; dads kneeled;

Have you ever made a journey by railway sleeping-car? Have | 13 | 63
you known the excitement of settling down in a cosy bunk, to | 25 | 124
the rhythm of the wheels below, and waking up to a new | 36 | 179
landscape flashing by the carriage windows? | 45 | 225

For most people, travel by railway sleeper is a thing of the | 57 | 287
past, and long rail journeys are rare even by day. The car, | 70 | 348
the coach and the plane have largely taken over. Perhaps | 81 | 407
already the railway sleeper is just a fading memory. | 92 | 459

Passage 2 *SI 1.38*

Many typists and secretaries find good jobs abroad, often on | 12 | 62
contract to a foreign firm for a fixed period of time. Since | 25 | 125
English is so widely used throughout the world, it is not | 37 | 184
essential to be able to speak and write a second language | 48 | 242
though it is a great help. High speeds and standards in | 60 | 300
office skills are demanded - and met, since competition for | 72 | 360
good jobs abroad is keen. Many young people enjoy life | 83 | 417
abroad in this way as it gives them a chance to travel and | 95 | 476
see places they might not otherwise visit. | 104 | 518

Passage 3 *SI 1.35*

Proverbs express truths or wise sayings in familiar and | 11 | 57
often colourful ways. To say that the grass is always | 23 | 113
greener on the other side means that we always tend to feel | 35 | 173
our neighbour is more fortunate than we are; and of course | 46 | 232
he thinks the same about us. | 52 | 262

The saying that he who hesitates is lost is a warning against | 65 | 325
not being able to make up our mind. To be told to look | 76 | 382
before you leap is advice against rashness. Although these | 89 | 443
may seem to conflict, they are really only saying that there | 101 | 504
are times for bold decision and times for caution. Proverbs | 113 | 566
enrich our language and it would be the poorer without them. | 125 | 626

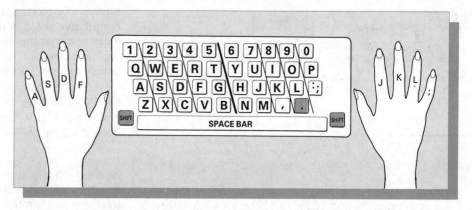

Two spaces after a full stop.
One space after ; and : Always start with warm-up practice.

Shift keys

These two large keys at the bottom are used for typing capital letters. When typing a left-hand capital letter, use the right-hand shift key, and vice versa.

For left-hand capitals (line 1)
1 Hold down the right-hand shift key with right-hand little finger.   Depress
2 Type required letter with the left hand.   Strike
3 Return the right little finger to its home key.   Release

For **right-hand** capitals (line 9) use opposite hands to the above.

Left-hand capitals
(use right shift key)

1 fF; Fan; Fell; Fake; dD; Dan; Dell; Dad;
2 sS; Sand; Sell; Sad; aA; Ale; Ash; Anne;
3 gG; Gall; Gene; Gale; eE; End; Elk; Eel;

4 Sell; Dan; Ale; Fan; Dean; Elf; A; Gale;
5 All seed; Dead end; Sea shell; Gas leak;

use L finger

6 ll. ll. ll. l.. l.. l.. l.l l.l l.l l..l
7 Sell a hen. Deal a hand. End all gags.
8 Add sea shells. Gag lags. Fake a lead.

Right-hand capitals
(use left shift key)

9   jJa Jag; Jen; Jake; kKa Ken; Kale; Keen;
10 lLa Lake; Len; Lad; hHa Hag; Heel; Hand;
11 nNa Nag; Neal; Nan; ;:a Leg: Jane: Held:

12 Handle shells. Lend nags. Keg all ale.
13 Jag lads. Nan sells jade. Lend a hand.

Revise all keys learned

14 Jan feeds hens; and sells eggs and kale.
15 Deanna has a keen sense: and lean hands.

Accuracy/speed timings of 4, 6, 8 and 10 minutes

In these longer A/S timings you will no longer follow the 4-step practice, and you should correct your errors by the quickest effective method on your machine. Uncorrected errors should be ringed as in the 1 and 2 minute timings.

1 **Gross Speed and Net Speed** From now on you must link accuracy and speed more closely. You will measure *Gross Speed* (over the full extent of your typing regardless of the number of uncorrected errors) and *Net Speed* (disregarding everything typed after the error cut-off point based on an error allowance of one error per 2 minutes, plus one overall). Thus the following error cut-off points apply.

    4 mins (3 errors allowed) Count up to and including word before 4th error.
    6 mins (4 errors allowed) Count up to and including word before 5th error.
    8 mins (5 errors allowed) Count up to and including word before 6th error.
    10 mins (6 errors allowed) Count up to and including word before 7th error.

2 **Counting Standard Words** The examination method will now be fully applied, ie adding one stroke for each extra key movement (use of shift key, carrier/carriage return, etc).

3 **Counting Gross Speed** At the end of each line of type of the passages that follow you are given the cumulative word count and stroke count. Take the word count at the end of the last complete line you typed: work out and add on the extra standard words for any part-line also typed. Divide the total by the number of minutes of the timing to find your Gross Speed in words per minute (wpm). For example, if you typed 140 standard words in 4 minutes, your Gross Speed was 35 wpm.

4 **Counting Net Speed** uses the same counting method – but you only count standard words up to the error cut-off point, as given above. Thus in the example just quoted, your typing would only count up to the 4th uncorrected error. *You should aim to keep your Gross Speed and Net Speed as close as possible*, which means aiming for the highest speed at which you can keep within the error allowance. Here the correction of errors factor comes into play.

5 **Record your results** on A4 forms like the one shown below. Type your own forms – and keep a different form (or column) for each length of timing.

6 **Set goals for Net Speed** At the start of the 4 minute timings, take the highest forced speed (in wpm) achieved in recent 2 minute timings as your Net Speed Goal. Work the following passages in rotation till your goal has been reached in them all, or in as many as your teacher instructs or you think fit. Then proceed to 6 minute timings and work the passages in the same way with a new Net Speed Goal. Finally proceed to 8 then 10 minute timings. In this way you will build up a solid foundation of accuracy combined with speed.

7 **Typing the passages**

a Copy the text exactly as given (line endings, capitalisation, etc).
b You may correct your errors
c If you finish the passage before the end of the timing, start it again.

Length of timings ....   Name ....
Class ....
Term ....

Date	Passage No	Gross Speed wpm	Net Speed wpm		Date	Passage No	Gross Speed wpm	Net Speed wpm
16 Jan	1	35	30					
18 Jan	2	37	32					

Aim for accuracy, fluency and speed. Prop up book so it slopes towards you.

I
use K finger

1 kki kki kki kii kii kii kik kik kik kiik
2 hike hikes hiked like likes liked did in
3 kill sill fill gill jail sail hail fails

4 Diana said killing inside jail is a sin.
5 Ian fails in singing: Gillian in hiking.

R
use F finger

6 ffr ffr ffr frr frr frr frf frf frf frrf
7 frail fried free rake rail reel reek ran
8 ark dark larks jerk dear near jeer sneer

9 Frieda likes fine rings and red dresses.
10 Fresh fish is dear and hares are dearer.

O
use L finger

11 llo llo llo loo loo loo lol lol lol lool
12 loll loss logs dog jog fog hogs rod hods
13 load loans loaf food hood good folk dose

14 Loss of good looks is no joke for Rosie.
15 Fresh roes on a long loaf are good food.

Revise all keys learned

16 Jones feared for his life on dark roads.
17 Idleness is foolish; learn a good skill.
18 Dense fog fell on hills and dales alike.
19 Old fools jeer: daring soldiers ride on.
20 Her girls like red roses and gold rings.

(Memo)

From Brian Cranford   To Louise Hacker
Ref PS/CF/5

CREDIT CARD LOSSES

Last month I recd a substantial number of enquiries from
new cardholders arising from our leaflet entitled (Typist - please
⊘ insert the title). Now may be ~~a good~~ ᵃⁿ ⁱᵈᵉⁿᵗ time to revise the
leaflet by incorporating a form ~~so that~~ ᵒⁿ ʷʰ immed application
can be made for protection against loss or theft of cards.

Can you rough out a simple form? I envisage the size being
approx 90 mm (3½ in) by 212 mm (8¼"). One side shd
contain a summary of the reasons for, & (developement) of,
our protection plan: use the existing leaflet to help
you.) ~~There may also be room for an illustration.~~

(The reverse shd have the (cardholders') name and address;
(single or joint)
(required) protection/; account number; sig & date lines; & our
Freepost return address.

Can we arrange a meeting for 2 pm on Thurs of next week,
(Typist — insert correct date) to discuss this matter?

Address a label to
Louise Hacker at
Praxigraphics PLC
67 Ancre Lane
LONDON SWIH 9HD

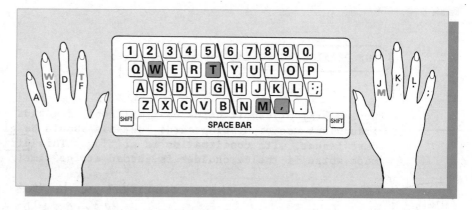

One space after colon, semi-colon and comma. Two spaces after full stop.

M
use J finger

1. jjm jjm jjm jmm jmm jmm jmj jmj jmj jmmj
2. jam jams jammed jamming elm gem hem hems
3. rim him dim dims dimming home some domes

4. Miriam made me more lime and lemon jams.
5. Mr Jim Hammond mends frames for farmers.

W
use S finger

6. ssw ssw ssw sww sww sww sws sws sws swws
7. swam was wall saw laws we well were when
8. swim swims swimming wise won woods wool;

9. Win will wed Owen Wise when work allows.
10. While walking in Wormwood we saw an owl.

T
use F finger

11. fft fft fft ftt ftt ftt ftf ftf ftf fttf
12. fat fate mat mate set jet let met it fit
13. kit kite dot lot not note foot loot seat

14. Thomas told a tall tale to Tessa Tinker.
15. Lottie took a rest while Katie made tea.

,
use K finger

16. kk, kk, kk, k,, k,, k,, k,k k,k k,k k,,k

Revise all keys learned

17. Sam, Kim and John were all good friends.
18. Make me an omelette, with milk to drink.
19. Her father is Danish, her mother German.
20. Jan wore a light dress: Kim a straw hat.
21. Mo told Wilma that the new jam was made.

THE PRAXIGUARD SCHEME — *Spaced caps*

(Stolen or lost) credit cards cost millions of pounds each year. To prevent fraudulent use of missing cards, details should be given quickly to each card issuer, with confirmation in writing. This (dificult) situation is made worse if the cardholder is abroad at the time!

Double or 1½ line spacing for these paragraphs please.

We bel that we have the solution to this problem. For a small annual sum you can join our PRAXIGUARD SCHEME ~~wh means that,~~ *whereby,* in the event of loss or theft, we undertake to inform yr card issuers immed by telex or telephone, drawing yr personal details from our confidential computer files. [We gntee up to £300 in claims for fraudulent use of yr cards if you advise us immed of their loss. The scheme provides further, substantial benefits for you.

Inset these numbered paragraphs from the margin please.

1 EMERGENCY FUNDS

Lost cards can lead to your becoming stranded without sufficient finance. If necessary, we will advance you an interest-free loan of two hundred pounds, and arrange travel tickets from anywhere in the world.

2 MEDICAL HELP

~~Accidents or illnesses abroad can mean extra difficulties.~~ The PRAXIGUARD SCHEME allows for expert medical attention abroad and for your swift and safe return by airambulance to the UK.

3 PROPERTY PROTECTION

We record the serial numbers of your ~~valuable possessions~~ *valuables* and important documents so that if these become lost or stolen, identification and proof of ownership would rapidly be provided for insurance companies and police.

4 ANTI-THEFT LABELS

Attached to the reverse of your cards, these act as a warning to would-be (theives) that you belong to a card protection scheme.

Leave 4 clear line spaces here.

An application form and details of further PRAXIGUARD SCHEME benefits can be obtained from Praxiteles Group Praxiteles House Adam Street LONDON WC2N 6AJ.

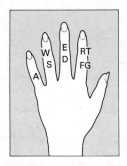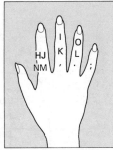

One-line sentences

1 Get me a tin of milk from the new store.

2 We will see the old film this afternoon.

3 If it rains, meet Harold in the shelter.

4 Edith likes to make flower arrangements.

Longer sentences

5 Ann wrote her friend, Jim, a long letter
telling him all she had seen in Ireland.

6 It is good to see foreign goods on offer
here, while we sell lots in other lands.

7 Martha likes sewing and has made herself
skirts and hats as well as other things.

8 Whilst all golfers like the game in warm
weather, some are as keen in winter too.

9 Her friends, Kate and Joan, are going to
join the Fen Tennis Team that was formed
in Newtown at the wish of John S Harman.

Blocked paragraphs

10 If we go home tired from work, the first
thing we do is rest. After that we take
a stroll and then it is time for dinner.

11 We had to wait indoors all the afternoon
as it rained so hard and the wind was so
wild. Later on, we went to the theatre.

12 When all is said and done, this regiment
was one of the finest. While others won
more medals, none won more lasting fame.

Carriage/carrier returns
(really speed it up)

13 We
We will
We will see
We will see her
We will see her tomorrow.

BJC/CA1004/DIS

PERSONAL

Mrs S H Markham
47 Lansdowne Ave
NEWPORT
Gwent
NP9 7QP

Typist — 2 carbon copies please — one for N C Peel and one for the file.

Dr Mrs Markham

In the event of ~~you losing yr credit cards~~ yr credit cards being lost or stolen, to prevent fraud you must inform each card issuer, ~~asap~~ by telephone, of yr ~~card~~ ~~account~~ number & their expiry date. You must then confirm these details in writing.

By investing a small annual sum in our PRAXIGUARD ~~PROTECTION~~ SCHEME, yr/confidential details are stored in our computer and if yr cards are lost or stolen, one telephone call wl ensure that all issuers are informed. Replacement cards wl be arranged & insurance cover provided for poss claims arising from any misuse of yr cards.

The enclosed/PRAXIGUARD SCHEME leaflet gives full details of all benifits. If we can be of further help, please contact us again.

Yrs scly

B J Cranford
Insurance Consultant

Address a label to Mrs Markham please.

Accuracy and speed must be developed together. Slow fingering can become largely a matter of *habit*. The specific object of the one and two minute A/S passages (Units 9 to 44) is to compel your fingers to move faster, with accuracy. You will not correct errors in one and two minute timings.

Counting your speed Words are counted as 'standard' words of five 'strokes', each letter and space counting as one stroke. Thus in a typing line of 50 strokes there are 10 standard words, regardless of the number of actual words. The scale beneath each A/S passage divides the line into standard words to help you count how many standard words you typed (see line 20 in Unit 9). Therefore if you typed exactly 2½ lines, you typed 25 standard words.

Before starting A/S timings, type the passage at least once to gain familiarity. Keep the 4 steps clearly separated as illustrated below.

Step 1 (Control) Type for *exactly* one minute aiming for reasonable accuracy. Ring each word that contains one or more errors (faults in spacing and punctuation marks count as part of the preceding word). Count the standard words typed. Write in the margin C for Control followed by the number of ringed words and, in brackets, the number of standard words typed, eg C2 (15).

Step 2 (Increase speed) Type again for one minute, increasing speed even though you make more errors. Count the standard words typed and write this with an S for Speed in the margin, eg S 22. (Ignore errors).

Step 3 (Force speed) Type again for one minute, pushing your speed still higher. Count the standard words typed and write this as in Step 2, eg S26. (Ignore errors.)

Step 4 (Control) Type again for one minute, aiming for accuracy. Ring your errors and count the standard words typed. Write the results as in Step 1, eg C1 (19).

Your final one minute of typing should be *both faster and more accurate* than your first one. Your confidence will grow, and your accuracy and speed will improve in all your work. Your teacher will control A/S training. On your own, you can time yourself with a stop-watch — but it is better to get someone else to do it for you.

Your first A/S practice (Unit 9) may look like this.

(Step 1)	When the sun (shuhes,) he likes to work in the open. When the (sjn) shines, he li	C 2 (15)
(Step 2)	When the sjn shines, he liked to work in the open. When the sun shines, he likes to wirk in the open. Whej the s	S 22
(Step 3)	When the sun shines he liked to work in the open. When the suj shines, he likes to work in the open. When the sun shines, he likes	S 26
(Step 4)	When the sun shines, he likes to work in the open. When the sun shines, (hd) likes to work in the op	C1 (19)

Recording your performance (devise a suitable form on A4 paper)

Date	A/S No	Length of Timings	First Control Timing	Highest Speed Timing	Final Control Timing
26 May	1	1 min	C2 (15)	S 26	C1 (19)
28 May	2	1 min	C2 (18)	S 27	C1 (22)

Proofreading Use your A/S training to pay *special attention* to checking your typescript. Check letter for letter and space for space. If in your final one minute of typing you make more than one error, look to see whether any letter is causing particular trouble. If it is, go back to the page where it was first introduced, for additional practice. When you have covered the complete alphabet (Unit 11) you can use the intensive letter practice given in the Error Clinic in Unit 13. As often as possible, get someone else to check your A/S checking (in a class, change papers).

Change all instances of "papers" to "articles"

INFORMATION TECHNOLOGY JOURNAL (TO BE PUBLISHED QUARTERLY)

FIRST ISSUE TO BE PUBLISHED JANUARY 1987

TYPIST - leave 2·5cm (1") ↑

THE

INVITED PAPERS TO BE INCLUDED IN ∧ FIRST ISSUE ARE

• • • Word Processing packages compared
• • • Databases – An ~~introductory~~ step-by-step guide to Omnibase
• • • Spreadsheets – What's new on the Market?
• • • Small Business Computers – Inside the Scythe kneetop
• • • Peripherals – desktop laser printer
• • • The Electronic Office

Use any typing method to highlight the words "Chief Editor" wherever they appear

REGULAR FEATURES TO INCLUDE

• • • Educational Newsletter
• • • Readers' Microcomputer Problem Pages
• • • Computer Companies' News Page

OFFERS OF PAPERS TO BE SUBMITTED TO

Chief Editor
Mr David Murray

Praxiteles Group
Adam Street
LONDON
WC2N 6AJ

An International Editorial Advisory Board has been assembled who w/ assist the Chief Editor in assessing papers. // A detailed guide to presentation of papers is under preparation.

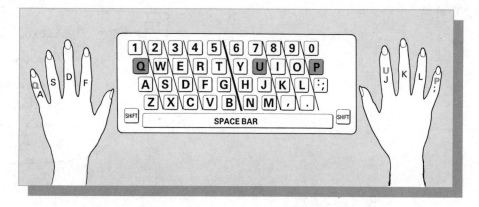

New left margin for Units 9–11: Pica 15, Elite 25.
In A/S work (see line 20 below) SI means syllabic intensity (the average number of syllables in the actual words).

P
use semi-colon finger

1 ;;p ;;p ;;p ;pp ;pp ;pp ;p; ;p; ;p; ;;p ;pp ;p; pp
2 lap; sap; pads; spade; spades; weep; sweep; sweeps
3 sip; lip; pin; pride; kipper; fop; lop; sop; rope;

4 Pam slipped pen, paper and an apple into the pram.
5 In the sprint, he pipped his opponent at the post.

U
use J finger

6 jju jju jju juu juu juu juj juj juj jju juu juj uu
7 jug jut just jute dull hull full pull gull sun nun
8 sung hung dust must rust pun fun hum rum sum under

9 For supper Lulu pulled jugfuls of pure pump water.
10 Our Aunt Una just put lumps of turnip in our soup.

Q
use A finger

11 aaq aaq aaq aqq aqq aqq aqa aqa aqa aaq aqq aqa qq
12 quakes quads squares squeals quell requests queens
13 quit quire require quote quota liquor equal equate

14 Quentin lent me a quaint square hat, with sequins.
15 The frequent request of the Quakers was for quiet.

Revise and test

16 In his wig and gown, the judge stood up and spoke.
17 More than a quarter of the students took the test.
18 This afternoon, Kim will go to a department store.
19 The order is: girls to remain indoors; lads to go.

S1 1.09

A/S 1 (1 minute)

20 When the sun shines, he likes to work in the open.

| 1| 2| 3| 4| 5| 6| 7| 8| 9| 10|

Typist - 1 Retain all abbreviations.
2 Change 15% to 14% throughout.
3 Please re-arrange the table so that the ONE YEAR block comes first, then FIVE YEARS and finally TEN YEARS.

PRAXILAZE

LOAN REPAYMENTS[1]

Period of loan	Your ~~Interest~~ payments		Monthly repayments per £1000
	Total interest ~~payable~~ per £1000	Total payable per £1000	
	£	£	£
TEN YEARS			
10% (APR 12·4%)	581·04	1581·04	13·17
12% (APR 14·7%)	714·30	1714·30	14·85
15% (APR 17·0%)	851·73	1815·73	15·44
FIVE YEARS			
10% (APR 14·1%)	272·64	1272·64	21·21
12% (APR 16·4%)	331·26	1331·26	23·19
15% (APR 18·8%)	391·41	1391·41	22·19
ONE YEAR			
10% (APR 27·9%)[2]	54·54	1054·54	87·88
12% (APR 30·5%)	65·59	1065·59	88·80
15% (APR 33·1%)	76·59	1076·59	89·72

Typist - make the style of this block the same as the others

1 Other years and interest rates available on request
2 Loan rate = Base Rate + 2%

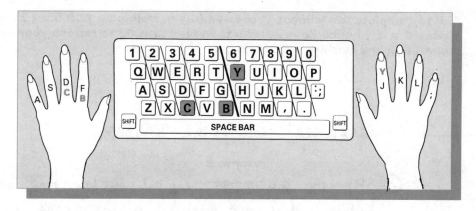

Always remember warm-up practice at start of typing.

B
use F finger

1 ffb ffb ffb fbb fbb fbb fbf fbf fbf ffb fbb fbf bb
2 fab jab dab ban ball web pebble bell fib fibs nibs
3 rib bid bib big fob sob lob mob boss dub rub bulbs

4 Babs and Billie liked to blow big, bright bubbles.
5 His big brother built a barn in timber and pebble.

Y
use J finger

6 jjy jjy jjy jyy jyy jyy jyj jyj jyj jjy jyy jyj yy
7 jay jays day days pays paying yawn yap yes yet yen
8 grey prey fry frying joys boys soya you your yours

9 Buy as many yards in red as they say you may need.
10 By day you may see my boy at play with young Gary.

C
use D finger

11 ddc ddc ddc dcc dcc dcc dcd dcd dcd ddc dcc dcd cc
12 decks pecks sack hack crack lice rice diced priced
13 cock mock sock lock suck luck ducked cycled crocks

14 Acrobatic clowns cycle in circles in circus rings.
15 Carrying coals to Newcastle causes constant chaos.

Revise and test

16 It is just a saying: when in doubt, best left out.
17 Queen Karen came in splendour to the royal palace.
18 James is the young club leader; Kenneth helps him.
19 Philip was bored by it all, and yawned frequently.

S1 1.08

A/S 2 (1 minute)

20 I hope to hear from you soon in answer to my note.

Task 1

PRAXILAZE TIME-SHARE HOLIDAYS

✓ Although the ~~initial~~ original capital outlay may seem substantial, we believe that our offer of a luxurious holiday EVERY YEAR FOR THE NEXT 10 YEARS is well worth your investment.

A single payment from just £600 ensures an annual luxury holiday ~~for you and your family.~~

[Typist – use any method to emphasise this paragraph] At the end of this 10-year period the whole of your initial payment will be returned to you.

[Typist – leave a space here 64 mm (2½ in) by 51 mm (2 in) for illustrations to be put in.]

If you do not wish to use your accommodation, take advantage of our world-wide exchange scheme – America, the West Indies, southern Europe. Alternatively, allow us to let it for you.

The luxuriously furnished and equipped apartments overlook an attractive bay.

There are many amenities within the complex – health centre, (sun patio,) and swimming pool sporting facilities, restaurant and coffee shop.

The project has attracted ~~much interest~~ many enquiries and, as apartments are obviously limited, we would advise early application.

Are you looking at the keyboard as little as possible? Is your sitting position correct and comfortable (see page 3)?

V
use F finger

1 ffv ffv ffv fvv fvv fvv fvf fvf fvf ffv fvv fvf vv
2 rave have gave ever lever dive jive live dove move
3 van vat vet vile villa vow valid very value vipers

4 Each villa has a very lovely view over the valley.
5 Sylvia and Vic have voices of average vocal value.

X
use S finger

6 ssx ssx ssx sxx sxx sxx sxs sxs sxs ssx sxx sxs xx
7 ax lax wax sex exit six mix fox box oxen crux flax
8 tax taxes taxi exist extra fixed mixed boxes boxer

9 The expert boxers were vexed at these extra taxes.
10 Rex used an axe to fix an extra post at each exit.

Z
use A finger

11 aaz aaz aaz azz azz azz aza aza aza aaz azz aza zz
12 laze lazy craze crazy size sizes dozen frozen buzz
13 zero zeal zip zinc zoo zoom fuzzy zebra azure haze

14 The crazy zealots had fuzzy hair and blazing eyes.
15 Zaza says that zeal brings endless zest to living.

Revise and test

16 If he follows the instructions he cannot go wrong.
17 Every customer has the right to expect politeness.
18 We must avoid such mistakes in the final accounts.
19 Bill should jump quickly over the gate of the zoo.

SI 1.10

A/S 3 (1 minute)

20 The water from the pump was cool, pure, and clear.

| 1| 2| 3| 4| 5| 6| 7| 8| 9| 10|

While

~~t~~hese categories are not a gntee of wear, they do provide some useful guidance. The classification is by an expert industrial panel, using suitable criteria such as pile density and nature of fibre.

The purchaser can *therefore* feel some confidence in being guided by it in the choice of an Axminster, Wilton or Tufted carpet to serve a particular requirement. For example, a Category 4 carpet cd reasonably be expected to last longer than one from Category 3 in the living room or on the stairs. [Finally, there are some simple checks which purchasers can [make [themselves].

(Typist — one line of space between points)

i Samples can be compared by bending them over and seeing how much the carpet gapes. The more easily the backing can be seen through the pile, the less dense the pile is.

(GAPES)

ii Gently tugging at a few tufts will show whether they are firmly anchored.

iii Scrutiny of the backing will show how close the weave is — a closer weave lasts longer. ↓

I hope this information will be of some use to you.

Yrs scly

✓ It will also show whether the threads are straight & at right angles, ~~as they shd be~~. This makes for a stable backing, which helps to keep the carpet's shape.

P S Conversions
1 metre = 1.1 ~~sq~~ yard approx
1 sq m = 1.2 sq yard approx
Carpet costing £5 a sq yard wd cost about £6 a sq m

Tabulation

New left margin (for 60-stroke line): Pica 10, Elite 20 (Units 12 to 27).

Keep your typing of this Unit for error analysis in Unit 13. Proofread your work and ring each word that contains one or more errors, in the usual way.

Warm-up drill
(*whole alphabet*)

1   The crazy pavement was quickly fixed by a jolly old gardener.

Blocked paragraphs

2   In typing there are three different kinds of paragraph. They are called blocked, indented and hanging paragraphs.

3   Blocked paragraphs are the easiest and fastest to type; all lines begin at the same scale point. With blocked paragraphs in single spacing, as shown here, one line of space is left between paragraphs. Between blocked paragraphs in double spacing, one extra line of space must be left to show clearly where a new paragraph starts.

The tabulator pre-sets points along the typing line where you wish to stop. Applications include indenting paragraphs and setting out figures in columns. There are 3 tabulator controls: find them on your typewriter.

1   Tab set key to fix tab stops.
2   Tab clear key to clear tab stops.
3   Tab bar (or key) to move direct to the tab stops in turn.

To clear a tab stop, move to the tab stop position and press the tab clear key. Some machines have a device for clearing all tab stops at once.

Setting a tab stop for indented paragraphs The first line of an indented paragraph begins 5 spaces to the right of its other lines, and a tab stop should be used for it.

1   Clear all existing tab stops.
2   Tap space bar 5 times from left margin position.
3   Press the tab set key to fix a tab stop at this point.

Use the tabulator to type the indented paragraphs that follow. Type them first in single spacing as shown, then in double spacing (selector at 2). Finally, type again the blocked paragraphs given above. This time use double spacing.

Indented paragraphs

4   With indented paragraphs typed in single spacing, as shown here, one line of space is left between paragraphs. One line of space is also left between indented paragraphs in double spacing: the indentation clearly shows where new paragraphs begin.

5   You can now type both blocked and indented paragraphs. Later on you will learn how to type hanging paragraphs, where the first line of each paragraph starts two spaces to the left of the other lines. These are used far less often than blocked and indented paragraphs.

SI 1.17

A/S 4 (1 minute)

6   When you type, you should keep your eyes mainly on the copy.

| . | 1| | 2| | 3| | 4| | 5| | 6| | 7| | 8| | 9| | 10| | 11| | 12|

- **1 Warm-up drill**
  (alphabet/
  space bar)

  a b c d e f g h i j k l m n o p q r s t u v w x y z

- **2 Use an A4 letterhead to type the following two-page letter in the fully-blocked style.**

Ref CJB/CAB/2460

Miss Norah Long
Citizens Advice Bureau
Manston CAMBRIDGE CB2 4BS

This is a useful guide to the softness & warmth of the texture.

Dear Miss L —

INTELLIGENT CARPET BUYING

You asked whether I cd let you hv ~~some~~ any information th wd be helpful tr people who seek advice on buying carpets. There is of course a wide range of quality of materials & of manufacture, but here are some points the Purchaser can look out for. [Every carpet must be labelled with a clear indication of the ~~fibt~~ fibre content, eg 80% wool, 20% nylon. [In addition, those mfrs who are members of the British Carpet Manufs Association are required to grade their pile carpets a/c tr an agreed scheme, and tr show the classification on a British Carpet Mark affixed tr the carpet. The ~~gradings~~ categories are as follows.

Typist — one line of space between categories

1 Light domestic — eg bedrooms & secondary rooms with light traffic

2 Medium domestic and/or light contract

3 General domestic and/or medium contract

4 Heavy domestic and/or general contract - for all heavy domestic situations, like well-used living rooms, halls & main stairs

5 Heavy contract

L Luxury use - usually a long pile carpet of a quality better than Category 3, but not necessarily suitable for all traffic areas

Errors: Analysis and action

To know your mistakes is part of the way to rectifying them. Look at your typing of Unit 12. You have ringed your errors and should now complete the error checklist below (copy or photocopy it).

Put a cross in the appropriate column for every wrong letter or punctuation mark, each time it occurred.

Error checklist

Date						
A						
B						
C						
D						
E						
F						
G						
H						
I						
J						
K						
L						
M						
N						
O						
P						
Q						
R						
S						
T						
U						
V						
W						
X						
Y						
Z						
,						
.						
;						
:						

Now rectify your weaknesses and build up strengths by practice on the two pages of drills that follow. Repeat the above procedure periodically during your course.

Continuation sheets

1 **Letters with continuation sheet(s)** As a general rule, leave one inch (six lines of space) at the foot of the first page of the letter (make a pencil mark approximately one inch from the bottom as a guide).
2 Take to the continuation sheet *at least* two lines of text above the complimentary close or signature block (this may necessitate more than one inch being left at the foot of the first page).
3 There is no need to type PTO (please turn over), Contd (continued) or Over/ at the foot of the first page. But if instructed to do this, leave half an inch (3 lines of space) before typing it to finish flush with the right-hand margin.
4 Use matching plain paper for continuation sheet(s).
5 Use the same left and right margins as on the first page.
6 On the continuation sheet, leave a top margin of ½ inch before typing the continuation sheet details (which help to keep the letter as a whole together).
   a *fully blocked style* Type the page number, date, and name only of the addressee at the left margin, each on a separate line, in single spacing.
   b *semi-blocked style* Type the continuation sheet details all on one line where possible – the name of the addressee at the left margin, the page number in the centre, and the date finishing flush with the right-hand margin.
   (Both (*a*) and (*b*) are illustrated below)
7 Then leave ½ inch before continuing the text of the letter.

- 1 **Warm-up drill**
  (reaches br/rb)

  brag barb brew garb sabre curb fibre arbour bribe verb brunt

- 2 **Use plain A4 paper and the above guidelines to type the following continuation sheet to a fully-blocked letter.**

  ```
  2
  18 May 19--
  Mrs T Whitehouse


  and Mr Smithson will, as you request, call to see you and inspect the
  property next Monday morning at 11 am.  He will advise you concerning
  price and will elaborate further on the current difficulty of selling
  properties in the Kenwood locality.


  Yours faithfully
  UNIVERSAL ESTATE AGENTS




  J Smith
  Office Manager
  ```

- 3 **Use plain A4 paper and the above guidelines to type the following continuation sheet to a semi-blocked letter.**

  ```
  Mrs T Whitehouse                2                    18 May 19--


  and Mr Smithson will, as you request, call to see you and inspect the
  property next Monday morning at 11 am.  He will advise you concerning
  price and will elaborate further on the current difficulty of selling
  properties in the Kenwood locality.

                                  Yours faithfully
                                  UNIVERSAL ESTATE AGENTS



                                  J Smith
                                  Office Manager
  ```

A as an at and are bad can say data saga abate agate
Sarah and Alastair said that all was black at sea.

B fbf fbf be by bar bib babe bomb abbey abbot bubble
Babs obeyed but big Bob Robbins rebuked both boys.

C dcd dcd can act cut ice cash fact back crack cocoa
Selecting rich cream cake, Dick cut choice slices.

D do dad did dog dig had made laid dared added dated
Do send Donald Dodds today and avoid added damage.

E ded ded let eat eel fee ease else even lever lease
When we see three silver beech trees we are there.

F if of off far fly fir for fix safe left fear fifth
Effie Cliff feared for her life if foxes followed.

G fgf fgf gap leg ago gag gave gift page going aging
Ginger George gave the giggling girls a great hug.

H jhj jhj had his her has have help hope share hatch
Hugh Sharp thought the Houghton Heath church high.

I kik kik aim him lip pit live mine mini faint livid
Willis printed his initials in ink inside the lid.

J jag jar jug job jack ajar jerk junk joke jump just
Juicy jam and jelly are his joys in June and July.

K key kid kit ask ink kick knee knot kink work knack
Kay Borkovski likes to take her book back quickly.

L lay let lid lot old last leak lily lift loll level
Lulled by low melodies, Willie fell slowly asleep.

M jmj jmj map may met arm move harm main madam impel
Tommy Mitchell mimed Miriam impromptu from memory.

N jnj jnj any not win can send seen none known inner
In noon sunshine Nanette gently nodded and snored.

O lol lol oak ore oar off coal sold solo folio motor
Dorothy took good photos from our top room window.

P ;p; ;p; pay peg pig top open upon stop paper upper
Pippa promptly propped up her puny apple saplings.

Q aqa aqa quay quite quiet quest quota squad quality
Raquel quietly requests an equal quota of sequins.

R frf frf red rob bar art rare roar rear razor error
Rory Roper thrice reared three rare brown rabbits.

S as is us so say saw sit sum use sun sure sews sows
As soon as is safe, ask Susie Spiers to assist us.

> **Semi-blocked letters** Although the fully-blocked letter style is widely used, some variations are favoured by different businesses. In an office you would be expected to conform to the house-style. One variation is shown below. Note the following points.
>
> *a* Date on same line as the reference, finishing at the right-hand margin. Use the right align function *or* backspace from the right-hand margin.
> *b* Centred subject heading.
> *c* Indented paragraphs.
> *d* *Signature block* Each line begins at a tab stop set approximately half-way across the typing line.

- **1 Warm-up drill**
  (figures)

  a1 s2 d3 f4 f5 j6 j7 k8 19 ;0 a1 s2 d3 f4 f5 j6 j7 k8 19 ;0

- **2 Use A4 letterhead * use the semi-blocked style outlined above.**

Ref JTS/PRS/1873   24 May 19--

For the attention of Mr A J Macrae

Messrs Martin & Macrae
24-26 Loganlea Rd
GLASGOW G4 8OT

Dear Sirs

SPECIAL OFFER IN CARPETING

In yr last quarterly circular ~~to customers~~ you announced ✓ that you wd be offering special terms for a wide range of (this month) carpeting. Please quote yr lowest prices for the following:-

100 m × 4 m wool carpeting, Star Quality
100 m × 3 m carpeting, 80% wool, 20% nylon
50 m × 4 m Supreme Cord carpeting

Kindly send samples & sales literature. Please also confirm that you can deliver within 4 wks of receipt of an order.

Yrs ffly
UNIVERSAL CARPETS LIMITED

Julius Sim
Purchasing Manager

- **3 Type again the letter in Unit 129 * use the same semi-blocked style given above.**

- **4 Type again the letter in Unit 130 * use the same semi-blocked style given above.**

T   ftf ftf tap the put out part tape stop treat stoat
Try to attract their attention with a toy trumpet.

U   juj juj use our you buy unit full burn union usual
You must surely guard such a full, valuable purse.

V   fvf fvf vast very over save give valve verve vivid
Vivien Volavka lives in clover in Lovesverry Vale.

W   sws sws was now who new what when were water white
When we want well water we walk to Swansdown Well.

X   sxs sxs axe tax box six exits exist excuse complex
Rex Baxter of Axminster fixed six extra wax boxes.

Y   jyj jyj any yes yet you year play rely reply early
Yes, try YESTERDAY for your yearly activity plays.

Z   aza aza size zinc zone zero maze azure blaze seize
No dazzling prize for zeal to lazy Suzy Zuckerman.

Comma a, b, c, d, e, f, g, h, i, j, k, l, m, n, o, p, q,
r, s, t, u, v, w, x, y, z, a, b, c, d, e, f, g, h,

Semi-colon a; b; c; d; e; f; g; h; i; j; k; l; m; n; o; p; q;
r; s; t; u; v; w; x; y; z; a; b; c; d; e; f; g; h;

Colon a: b: c: d: e: f: g: h: i: j: k: l: m: n: o: p: q:
r: s: t: u: v: w: x: y: z: a: b: c: d: e: f: g: h:

Full stop a. b. c. d. e. f. g. h. i. j. k. l. m.
n. o. p. q. r. s. t. u. v. w. x. y. z.

Space bar a b c d e f g h i j k l m n o p q r s t u v w x y z

Shift keys aA bB cC dD eE fF gG hH iI jJ kK lL mM nN oO pP qQ
rR sS tT uU vV wW xX yY zZ aA bB cC dD eE fF gG hH

Right shift key Ada Sue Dan Fay Gus Wynn Eva Rob Ted Zoe Bert Vera
Brenda Winterton was treated by Dr V C Quinn FRCS.

Left shift key Yul Una Ian Olly Pam Hugh Jim Kay Lily May Nanette
Major Percy K Hougham MP lives in Unity Nash Mews.

Carrier return Thank
Thank you
Thank you for
Thank you for your
Thank you for your letter.

Double letters We hope it will be possible for you to supply
immediately some additional jigsaw puzzles. They
have been a big success, real winners. We suggest
you send, as soon as possible, a further supply of
wooden puzzles in the cottage, poppy, and spinning
wheel patterns. We are sorry to rush you but are
finding it difficult to meet demand for these
excellent goods.

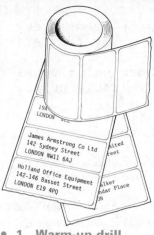

1 **Labels** of varying size are available in rolls or on sheets – for typing in series and sticking on envelopes.

2 Where a large number of identical circular letters is produced for posting to names and addresses on a given list, time is saved by using labels – and not having to put each envelope separately through the typewriter.

3 The labels are self-adhesive and attached to a special backing. When typed they are peeled off the backing one by one and suitably placed on the envelope.

4 Typed labels are, of course, necessary for padded Jiffy bags and packets.

● 1 **Warm-up drill**
(quotation marks)

The witness replied: "From my position behind the door, I heard the words 'shoot and run' immediately before he shot".

● 2 **Type the following circular letter on an A4 letterhead for eventual duplication * date as month and year only.**

Dr Householder

We are specialists in exterior protection & decorative coatings, & during the next few wks are viewing a number of properties in yr area to assist us in the advertising of our Protective Coatings. The type & location of yr property cd be of interest to our advertising project.

in full please — (UBMS) can completely [written] reface exterior walls, no matter what type of surface & condition. Amongst our varied treatments is Hy-Tex, which carries a 15-yr gntee. Hy-Tex is a technically controlled blend of minerals, resins, plastics & chemicals wh is 15 to 20 times thicker than conventional paint. It is applied at high pressure wh in effect welds the material to the wall surface, ~~providing an~~ ① ~~extremely durable coating~~ wh wl not chip, flake, or peel, prevents penetrating damp, resists heat, cold, & even corrosive salt sea winds.

We are able to offer high discounts to properties selected for our advertising project. All that is required in return is before and after photographs & to be able to use yr address so that prospective clients may view the finish (fr the outside only & with no personal inconvenience) & perhaps a letter of recommendation 12 mths after the installation.

We look forward to hearing fr you.

Yrs ffly   (space for signature)

John Stanley
Advertising Manager
(Universal Building Maintenance Systems)

[If you feel this offer may be of interest to you, please get in touch with us, without any obligation whatsoever.]

● 3 **Type three labels to the following:**

Mr & Mrs K White
64 Elm Close
DERBY DE6 4AG

Miss M Chapman
128 Birmingham Rd
Derby DE2 4GK

Mr S King
59 Silverdale Rd
Derby DE9 6PB

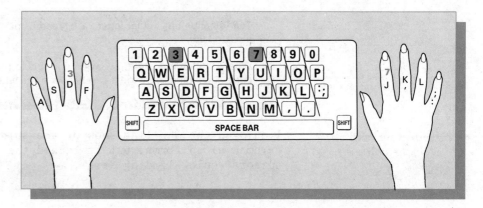

*Before typing a new figure, practise the finger movement as usual. When typing figures, look if necessary, but **always use the correct finger**.*

Warm-up drill
(*whole alphabet*)

1   The quick, brown fox jumped right over the lazy, black dogs.

3 *use D finger*

2   de3ed de3d d3d de3ed de3d d3d: 3 duds 33 dots 3 dons 33 dogs

7 *use J finger*

3   ju7uj ju7j j7j ju7uj ju7j j7j: 7 jugs 77 jars 7 jams 77 jigs

Practise 3 and 7

4   There were 737 seeds planted: but only 337 swedes took root.

5   Jack cut 73 cabbages, 7 marrows and 37 cucumbers in 3 weeks.

6   Sally moved from 3 Wood Road, London E7 to 73 Mill Lane, N3.

7   She baked 7 loaves, 3 jam rolls, 7 fruit cakes and 33 tarts.

8   On the farm there were 3 horses, 7 cows, 7 pigs and 33 hens.

9   I am 37 years old and my sons are 7 and 3. My father is 73.

10   In only 3 weeks I read 7 books ranging from 77 to 337 pages.

Revise and test
(*blocked paragraphs*)

11   During the heatwave, we sold a record number of 73 pairs of
     sandals in 3 days. Our previous best was 37 pairs in 3 days.
     That was nearly 7 years ago.

12   Mary says that 7 people will be coming on the picnic on
     3 August. We shall meet at my house at 37 Park Close, and
     drive the 37 kilometres to Beechwood Forest in 3 cars.

13   My lucky numbers are 3 and 7. My birthday is 3 July, and I
     am happy when the year has a 3 or a 7 in it. If possible, I
     always choose a raffle ticket like 33, 77, 37 or 73. When I
     moved to 77 High Street with its telephone number 73377, I
     felt my luck was in.

SI 1.17

A/S 5 (1 minute)

14   Be sure that you use the right finger when you type figures.

| | 1| 2| 3| 4| 5| 6| 7| 8| 9| 10| 11| 12|

1 **Tear-off slips** on circular letters are typed as on notices, advertisements, etc (Unit 95).

2 Where the letter is short, use wide margins to produce a well-balanced page — avoiding too wide a gap between the letter and the tear-off slip.

● 1 **Warm-up drill**
(*whole alphabet*)

I enjoyed the dazzling show of the soldiers in their vivid ceremonial uniforms, but it lacked the expertise of the sailors' quick-landing drill.

● 2 **Using an A4 letterhead, type the following draft circular letter with tear-off slip — aiming at good use of the available space.**

WP Assignment 10. *Key-in* document (CIRCULAR) for 10-pitch print-out. Subject heading and 'D Adams' (at foot) in bold. Use indent function to indent left and right margins for numbered section (or set new margins); and change to double spacing for this section. Use automatic paragraph numbering facility if available. Remember to use RETURN key at end of repeater key cut-off line and insertion lines. *Text-edit* Sentence 1: replace 'of a way' with 'how'. Start of sentence 2: delete 'The answer is', starting sentence with 'A water softener . . .' *Proof-read* text on screen, and correct. Print-out one copy in 10-pitch.

(date – give month + year)

Dear Householder

4 Steam irons + kettles last longer for the same reason.

A SOFT SOLUTION TO HARD PROBLEMS

At a time when all yr household bills are rising, let us tell you of a way you can hit back! The answer is a water softener which can help with many hard problems. Here are some:

1 It cuts down the amount of soap, shampoo + detergent you need to buy.

2 Clothes come softer from the wash + last longer: this applies particularly to woollens.

3 Maintenance + service costs are reduced on appliances like dishwashers + washing machines which can be ruined by hard water.

Complete + post at once / the coupon below. By return we wl send you / more information about water softeners.
to the above address
a lot

Yrs ffly

D Adams Marketing Manager

Name _____

Address _____

_____

_____

_____ Postcode _____

Warm-up. Unit 14 Paragraph 13. Check figure work extra carefully.

4 *use F finger*

1   fr4rf fr4f f4f fr4rf fr4f f4f: 4 figs 44 feet 4 fees 44 fans

8 *use K finger*

2   ki8ik ki8k k8k ki8ik ki8k k8k: 8 kits 88 keys 8 kids 88 kegs

Practise 4 and 8

3   Out of the 8 boys, 4 celebrated their 8th birthday on 4 May.

4   Bob has 48 flats to rent and 8 to sell: only 4 have garages.

Note the abbreviation for number

5   In order No 448 we asked for 4 pairs of gloves and 8 shirts.

6   The 8 crates contained 4 broken vases and 48 chipped plates.

7   Out of 848 buses, 48 broke down and 84 needed major repairs.

8   For a party of 8, we used 4 bottles of wine and 4 of sherry.

9   The new school will have 488 boys and 448 girls in 48 forms.

Revise and test
(*indented paragraphs*)

10   For homework, read pages 38 to 47 of your Office Practice textbook. Also, carefully check the answers to your work on page 34. Study the diagram on page 87 for a test in the next lesson.

11   During the storm which swept Seacroft for 48 hours, 7 houses were damaged by falling trees and 78 by flooding. In all, 343 people were left homeless. It will take at least 7 or 8 weeks to repair all the damage.

12   Go to the general store at 48 High Street and buy 3 bars of soap, 4 packets of biscuits, 7 tins of soup and 8 candles. Then, from the greengrocer at No 73 in the same street, buy 8 bananas, 7 oranges and 4 lemons. Take back the 3 bad apples they gave you yesterday.

SI 1.07

A/S 6 (*1 minute*)

13   It is much better to walk to the shops than to drive by car.

| 1| 2| 3| 4| 5| 6| 7| 8| 9| 10| 11| 12|

1 **Circular letters** Where a business sends out an identical letter in large numbers, this is known as a circular letter.

2 The copies may be printed or photocopied from a master. They may also be reproduced from the memory of an electronic typewriter or word processor, in which case individual salutations and inside names and addresses can, if desired, be included – by mail-merging from a separately stored list.

3 The date on circular letters may be shown as:

 a day, month and year – as on ordinary business letters (14 May 1988).
 b month and year only (May 1988)
 c Date as postmark.

● 1 **Warm-up drill**
 (reaches my/ym)

my hymn army nymph myth thyme myosis lymph myrrh rhyme mummy

● 2 **Type this letter to see how it will best fit on A4 headed paper * do not leave a space for an inside name and address or signature * keep an even right margin with word division * justify the right-hand margin if your machine has automatic justification.**

WP Assignment 9. *Key-in* document (WDISPLAY) for 10-pitch print-out. Use line-end word division and justify right-margin of body of letter. Subject heading and 'John Greening' (at foot) in bold. *Text-edit* Replace 'Date as Postmark' with current month and year of typing. Paragraph 3: delete 'entirely new and', also 'national and international' and 'in this field'. *Proof-read* text on screen, and correct. *Print-out* one copy in 10-pitch with justified right-margin.

Date as Postmark

← (2 lines of space)

Dear Careers Officer

ATTRACTIVE JOBS IN WINDOW DISPLAY

There wd be opps for working abroad ~~in this field~~ for young people who can speak French or German. ✓

I am writing in the hope that you may be able to help us in our search for creative young persons to undertake interesting Window Display Work in many of our shops. [As you may know, we are an international firm & trade in this country under the name of Fashion Leather & Fur. We concentrate mainly on ladies' and men's leather & suede garments (including shoes); also on all types of real fur. [We are currently embarking on an ~~entirely new &~~ imaginative programme to bring all our windows – & consequently our ~~national & international~~ image – right up to date.

We are very keen to involve in this venture young people with [flair & enthusiasm] for this sort of work. [If you feel that any of yr students might be interested in, & suitable for, this challenge then we shd be delighted & grateful if you wd let us know. We shall be pleased to arrange a local interview for anyone you recom. [Please ~~do not hesitate to~~ get in touch if you require any further details.

Yrs fly

Joan Greening

Display Director

(2 lines of space)

UNIT 130   Letters   Circular letters   **154**

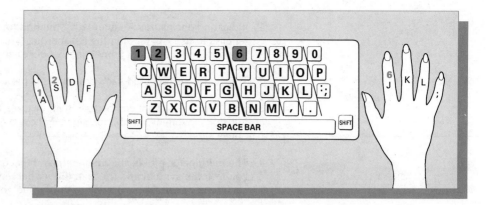

For figure 1, use only the figure 1 key – never small letter L or capital letter I.
Note that the comma is used as a thousand marker (but not in references, etc.)
See 11 and 12 below.

1 *use A finger*   1   aqlqa aqla ala aqlqa aqla ala: 1 aunt 11 arms 1 ally 11 ants

     2   Bring out 111 forks, 11 spoons and 1 bowl from the cupboard.

2 *use S finger*   3   sw2ws sw2s s2s sw2ws sw2s s2s: 2 saws 22 sons 2 suns 22 sets

6 *use J finger*   4   jy6yj jy6j j6j jy6yj jy6j j6j: 6 jays 66 jobs 6 jets 66 jabs

Practise 1 2 6   5   John hit 26 and 21 runs: Alan 61 not out in just 66 minutes.

     6   In the evening, 2 waiters and 6 waitresses served 61 guests.

     7   After work buy 6 lemons, 2 melons, 12 oranges and 16 apples.

     8   The 2 sums gave the same product: 2 times 66 and 6 times 22.

     9   Buses No 11, 12, 16, 61 and 62 all pass close to your hotel.

Revise and test
(*blocked paragrahs*)   10   Each of the following numbers can be evenly divided by 3 and 6: 6, 12, 24, 48 and 72. In addition, the last 3 numbers can be evenly divided by 8 and 12.

   11   As well as my home and office telephone numbers, 738412 and 31462, numbers which I carry in my head are my Cheque Card, 876117, and my Automobile Association membership number, 81 16144 182.

   12   In typing numbers, a single error can be critical. A letter sent to 126 instead of 216 Orchard Road could get lost. A reference quoted as 2136 instead of 2316 or a phone number given as 21624 instead of 21264 would be useless. In a business document, a mistype of 26,482 for 26,842 could be serious.

SI 1.05

A/S 7 (*1 minute*)   13   If you get a cheque card from your own bank you will be able to cash cheques at most banks.

| | 1| 2| 3| 4| 5| 6| 7| 8| 9| 10| 11| 12|

1 **Indicating enclosures** An alternative method to enc or encs at the foot of a letter is to use a symbol in the left margin, typed on the same line as the mention in the text that something is being enclosed.

2 The symbol is repeated each time there is mention of a new enclosure.

3 The marginal symbol can be one, two, or three (consistently) unspaced full stops, hyphens, or oblique signs. Follow the style in the copy or the house style.

4 The marginal symbols should line up with each other. Two spaces are left between the symbol and the text. (Either backspace into the left margin each time *or* set a tab stop where the symbol starts.

5 The marginal symbol method is useful to ensure that all enclosures are put in the envelope.

6 This method of indicating enclosures or attachments can also be used in memos.

● 1 **Warm-up drill**
(exclamation mark)

I'm coming! Quick, run! Watch that step! Please be quiet!
Help! All stand back! Goodness me! Oh shut up! Look out!

● 2 **The house-style for indicating enclosures is two full stops in the left margin.**

Our ref JGW/md/B796
Yr ref AB/jt/3056

J K Bonnette
Via Cassia Antica 96
I-00191 Roma
Italy
Dr Sirs
 YR ORDERS NO 3056 + 3057
We are sorry to hear that yr last consignment of books
contained the various damaged items that you hv returned.
Our credit note is enclosed. [We also regret that you had cause
to complain of late delivery. The delay resulted fr a dispute in
the printing trade.]
[Although this dispute is now settled, it will unfortunately take
some time for the printers to catch up w there arrears. [As
a result of this the following titles is missing from yr
latest order which is being separ despatched today, under
separate cover:
    The Story of North Sea Oil (Walters)
    European Furniture (Harrison)
    The Secret Agents (Hammond Press)
These wl be delivered to you as soon as they are
available — which shd be within the next 3 wks. [We
enclose a copy of our latest cat.
    Yrs ffly
UNIVERSAL PUBLICATIONS
John G Williams Despatch Dept

Check figure work figure for figure. When typing figures, look if necessary but always use the correct finger. Always use the figure key for 0, never capital letter O.

5 *use F finger*
9 *use L finger*
0 *use ; finger*

1   fr5rf fr5f f5f fr5rf fr5f f5f: 5 fins 55 fibs 5 fags 55 firs

2   lo9ol lo91 191 lo9ol lo91 191: 9 logs 99 lads 9 lots 99 laws

3   ;p0p; ;p0; ;0; ;p0p; ;p0; ;0; 20 pages; 30 pills; 400 papers

Practise 5 9 0

4   The 9 firms had 590 employees, 90 skilled and 500 unskilled.

5   His farm had 950 acres of wheat, 95 of oats and 5 of barley.

6   Order 90 locks and 95 keys for 90 doors in the 59 new flats.

7   Look for 5 or 55 for luck, but 50 or 950 will serve as well.

8   The 50 men built 9 houses, 9 garages and 5 shops in 90 days.

Revise and test
(*indented paragraphs*)

9   Ordinal numbers tell you about the order of things: 1st, 2nd, 3rd, 4th, 5th, and so on. Cardinal numbers tell you how many: 6, 7, 8, 9, 10, etc.

10   On the first 3 days of our tour we covered 375, 480 and 469 miles. This took us into the mountains, where 126 and 87 miles were as far as we cared to travel in the next 2 days. By a shorter return route we reached home in 2 daily stages of 485 and 469 miles.

11   Great care should be taken in typing and checking figures. Make this a habit with the small numbers which occur most often, like 6, 9, 10, 12 and 25. Then you are less likely to make mistakes with the larger numbers of 3 or more digits: 340 and 430, or 879 and 789 for instance.

SI 1.05

A/S 8 (*1 minute*)

12 When you use a shift key, be sure you do not release it till you have struck the right key.

  | 1| 2| 3| 4| 5| 6| 7| 8| 9| 10| 11| 12|

1 **Blind carbon copy** When it is unnecessary or undesirable for the addressee to know that a carbon copy has been distributed to other persons, this information is not given on the top copy of the letter. It is then known as a blind carbon copy.

2 When the letter has been typed, only the carbon copies (with appropriate carbon paper) are reinserted into the machine and the distribution typed on them, usually preceded by bcc – bcc Mrs G Finn
Mr S Grant

3 The carbon copies (including the file copy) are still marked in the usual way to ensure full and correct distribution.

4 There are times when only the originator should know to whom copies have been sent. Then the distribution list appears only on the file copy.

● 1 **Warm-up drill**
(brackets/
figures)

Results in £m (previous year in brackets). Turnover £1,039.5 (£1,010.1); profit before tax £181.0 (£191.9); profit after tax £123.2 (£145.3); dividends £39.0 (£39.0). Earnings per share 34.2p (39.84p); dividends per share 10.75p (10.75p).

● 2 **Take a carbon copy of this letter for Miss A. Henderson, Depository Manager (not to be shown on Mr Larsson's copy) * follow the above guidelines.**

WP Assignment 8. *Key-in* document (LETTER) for 12-pitch print-out. Use subject heading (in bold); FORTHCOMING HOUSE REMOVAL. *Text-edit* Paragraph 1 – amend date to third of next month (stating day of week and month); amend arrival time to 0830 hrs. *Proof-read* text on screen, and correct. *Print-out* 3 copies in 12-pitch.

Ref GD/CF

Mr G Larsson
24 Drummond Rd
BIRMINGHAM B16 2TX

Dr Sir / I confirm that we hv booked yr removal from yr address above to our Depository on the first of next month. Our van will arrive to begin loading at 0800 hrs. We have recd no instructions from you regarding insurance of goods while in transit or in store. We shd be pleased to ~~arrange~~ handle this as shown on the Estimate Form. We await your instructions on this matter — otherwise it is at owner's risk

Yrs ffly
G ~~Dawon~~ Dawson

You undertook to pack yr large quantity of books yourself, for this purpose & / we wl deliver 10 packing cases to yr address 2 days before the removal date.

1 **The date** can be typed in various ways. The recommended order is day, month, year – typed as 10 December 1988.

Dates all in figures can cause confusion between the day and month – 10.12.88 could be read as 10 December or October 12.

In future, *date all your work* to help keep it in the right order.

2 **The time** can be expressed in two ways – by the 12-hour clock method or by the 24-hour clock method.

   a With the *12-hour clock method*, a full stop is *always* used to separate hours and minutes, followed by am or pm (8.30 am, 2.45 pm, 7.05 pm).
   b With the *24-hour clock method*, there are always four digits – the first two giving the hour, the second two showing minutes after the hour. There is usually no stop separating the hours and minutes. The four figures are often followed by hours or hrs (0830 hrs, 1445, 1905 hours).

● **1 Warm-up drill**
(*figures*)

a1 s2 d3 f4 f5 j6 j7 k8 l9 ;0 a1 s2 d3 f4 f5 j6 j7 k8 l9 ;0

● **2 Type the two following sentences, first as shown, then a second time changing the 12-hour clock to the 24-hour clock and vice versa.**

From 20 December 1989 to 10 January 1990 the library will be open from 9.15 am to 4.45 pm Mondays to Fridays, and from 8.45 am to 12.30 pm on Saturdays.

My plane will arrive on 26 April at 0920 hrs: the others will follow on 27 April on the plane that arrives at 2030 hrs.

3 **Numbers as words or figures in continuous text**
   a There are no hard-and-fast rules. In business and technical documents the tendency is to use figures. In more literary documents the preference might be for words provided they are not too cumbersome.
   b In the absence of copy which you can follow (in Level 1 exams you should follow the copy) use this working method:

   Type all numbers as figures, but use words for numbers which start a sentence and for number one standing alone.

   c First or 1st, second or 2nd, third or 3rd, etc (ordinal numbers) – follow the copy, but ensure consistency throughout a document.

● **3 Type the two following sentences.**

In just one year the Company cut its manpower from 4,560 to 3,890, and yet increased its output from 27,000 to 29,000 units.

Whether ten or ten thousand people are likely to read my story, I shall write it as well as I can.

SI 1.18

● **4 Test**
A/S 9 (*1 minute*)

Most of the firms we questioned in our survey said that they planned to recruit more staff.

Letters

1 **Carbon copies for distribution** Sometimes a carbon copy of a letter, memo, etc, is sent to persons other than the addressee. (An additional carbon copy is always taken for the file.)

2 It is usual to show this at the foot of the letter by typing copy to or the abbreviation cc (for 'copy circulated to' or 'carbon copy to') followed by the name(s) of the other recipient(s). This is separated from the last typed item on the letter by at least one line of space.

3 To ensure full and correct distribution of the carbon copies, tick or underline on the carbon copy the name of the person for whom it is intended. The bottom carbon copy should be marked 'File' in the top right-hand corner.

● 1 **Warm-up drill**
   (question mark)

How many? What are they? How do you know? Must we all go? When? How? What do you mean? Do you see it? Can we come?

● 2 **3 carbon copies are needed of this letter * mark them as explained above to ensure they will be correctly distributed.**

Carbon paper
Top copy

Mr G Faulkner, 27 Park View Gdns, LONDON WC2C 7PN

Dr Mr Faulkner
At their mtg on Tues the Projects Cttee considerd yr manuscript of a book on the English Language and the EEC (title still to be decided). Mainly because of the excellent reports of the readers, it was warmly approved for publication in our list of books for next year. [Within the next 2 wks you shd receive a formal agreement. You will also rec a Promotion Folder from our Publicity Department for yr completion. [We are regarding this basically as an educational book, for Sixth Forms & Colleges, with a market in all the EEC countries + throughout the English-speaking world. [We are very happy to enter into association with you, as yr publisher.

Yrs scly

P White (Miss)
Educational Editor
cc Mr T Benjamin, Legal Department
   Miss P Light, Publicity Dept

WP Assignment 7. *Key-in* document (LETTER) for 12-pitch print-out. Use emboldened subject heading ENGLISH LANGUAGE BOOK. *Text-edit* in Mr Faulkner's address correct 'Gardens' to 'Terrace'. First line: insert 'Publication' in front of 'Projects'. End of paragraph 2: insert 'Kindly return these as soon as possible'. *Proof-read* text on screen, and correct. *Print-out* 4 copies in 12-pitch.

> 1 **Hyphen and dash** The same key is used for both. (Use the appropriate figure finger – otherwise the nearer little finger.)
>
> 2 The **hyphen** has no space before and after it. It is used:
>
>   *a* in words made up from two or more other words (first-class, up-to-date).
>   *b* to join together parts of a word (re-employ, non-existent).
>   *c* to represent the word 'to' (pages 91-96, 22-24 High Street).
>   *d* to divide words at the end of lines (See Unit 39).
>
> 3 The **dash** has one space before and one space after it. It may be used to mark off a comment or description in a sentence. There may be either a single dash or a pair.
>
>   Her work is now good - indeed excellent.
>   The old man - looking like a tramp - hobbled in.

● 1 **Warm-up drill**
(*whole alphabet*)

By just one reckless action in dropping a lighted match, an explosion and fire were caused which quickly razed the vast factory to the ground.

● 2 **Practise hypen**

In mid-February the sub-office will have a half-day holiday.

Sun-ray Cleaners moved from 6-8 Broadway to 18-20 High Road.

My father-in-law has a first-class job in Stratford-on-Avon.

● 3 **Practise dash**

Appearance matters at work - particularly in public offices.

When you return - I hope very soon - I shall show you round.

The conference will be in April - subject to Board approval.

● 4 **Revise and test**

There are 365 days in a year or 366 in a leap-year. Each year has 12 months - 7 with 31 days and 4 with 30 days. February has 28 days or 29 in a leap-year.

We were booked to join Flight XA 824 - due to leave London at 1456 hrs. With 80 passengers disembarking and 35 joining, the plane was 75 minutes late leaving London and 90 minutes late in arriving at our destination.

With their 2-stroke engines roaring, the motor-cycles of the Red Devil Gang sweep nightly through the ill-lit streets of Greentown - a danger to their riders and to passers-by alike. The local Anti-Noise League consider this gang a top-priority cause for action - since all their warnings have gone unheeded.

SI 1.31

● 5 **A/S 10** (*1 minute*)

We should be pleased to receive an early reply to the letter we sent to you last September.

| | 1| | 2| | 3| | 4| | 5| | 6| | 7| | 8| | 9| | 10| | 11| | 12| |

● 1 **Warm-up drill**
(carrier/
carriage
return)

Do
Do send
Do send them
Do send them at
Do send them at once.

● 2 **Use an A6 card.**

CONTACTING OUR OVERSEAS BRANCHES

Keep this table at hand to the ~~teph~~
telephone & consult it when wishing
to telephone overseas. It gives the
time difference, in hours, from GMT.

Retain abbreviation

New York	−5	Delhi	+5½
Munich	+1	Singapore	+7½ 8
Amsterdam	+1	Paris	+1
Athens	+2	Sydney	+10

Typist— alpha order please

● 3 **Use an A6 card.**

HAMPDEN PARK SPORTS CENTRE

Typist – rule square 1¾" × 1¾" (44 mm × 44 mm) for photograph

Name:

Membership No:

Date of issue:

Valid until:

Leave 2 lines of space between these items

This pass is issued subject to the rules & regulations
governing membership of Hampden Park Sports Centre.

1 **Symbols and signs**

   a These can differ in position on different machines. Always use the appropriate figure finger – otherwise the nearer little finger.

   b Continue to practise the finger movement from the home key before actually typing the new symbol or sign from the book.

   c You may look at the keyboard when typing these keys but *always use the correct finger*.

   d Carefully note and follow the spacing given.

2 **Apostrophe**

   a Shows possession, or omission of a letter.

   b Also serves for single quotation marks, which are interchangeable, with double quotation marks. (See Unit 21)

3 **@ sign**

This has limited uses. It should be used only in invoices and similar documents or in lists of items with prices.

4 **Typing from manuscript** (handwriting)

Always read through the whole paragraph before starting to type it – to become acquainted with the subject and handwriting. This will help you to read and spell all words correctly.

● **1 Warm-up drill**
(*hyphen*)

This 18-page leaflet contains an up-to-date list of all our full-time, part-time, and day-release courses in office skills subjects.

● **2 Practise** `'`

John's sister, Mary, is Vera's best friend. They are both in Mr Smith's class at Henderson's School. They couldn't join the school's athletics club last year because they weren't old enough.

● **3 Practise** `?`

What's the time? Where shall we go? Shall we walk or take the bus? Shall we be back by tea-time? If not, at what time shall we be back?

● **4 Practise** `@`

The account was made up as follows: 7 newspapers @ 25p each, 4 magazines @ 90p each, and 3 booklets @ 86p each.

● **5 Copy line by line**

I am writing to ask whether you received my letter which I
sent at the end of last month. I am rather concerned as I
have heard nothing from you, but the cheque I enclosed has
gone through my bank account. I should be glad to receive
an early reply.

● **6 Test**

A/S 11 (*1 minute*)

SI 1.26

People with indoor jobs should try to make it a rule to take exercise in the open each day.

| 1 | 2 | 3 | 4 | 5 | 6 | 7 | 8 | 9 | 10 | 11 | 12 |

- **1 Warm-up drill**
  (whole alphabet)   The zebra's very quaint stripes are just camouflage, an excellent blend with the background of tall grasses on the African plains.

- **2 Use an A6 card for the following itinerary:**

MR P PROWSE : at Company's Annual Dinner in London

Thursday , (Typist - put next Thursday's date here)

1700 hrs	Depart Peterborough Station
1815	Arrive London Kings Cross
1930	(for 2000 hrs) Dinner at Savoy Hotel
2345	Arrive Peterborough Station
2230	Depart London Kings Cross

Taxi ordered to drive you home from Peterborough Station

- **3 Use an A6 card for the following appointments schedule:**

MRS P WARD - APPOINTMENTS SCHEDULE

Friday (Typist - next Friday's date here)

0930 hrs	Dr C Bailey of SOFTWARE PRODUCT SERVICES LTD calling to discuss staff training (File J 207/CB).
1115 "	Senior Staff meeting in Board Rm — to be addressed by yrself & Dr Bailey.
1245 "	Lunch at SWAN HOTEL with Dr Bailey & Mr G White.
1430 "	Dr Bailey — SPS consultancy on Business Graphics & Resource Management.

1 **Oblique sign or solidus** (/)
This sign has limited uses. The main ones are shown below in 2.

2 **Ampersand** (&)
Its use in names and abbreviations is shown in 3 below. Except in such specific uses 'and' should be typed in full.

3 **Double quotation marks** (")
These can be used to enclose direct speech, and are interchangeable with single quotation marks (apostrophe). Sometimes both single and double are called for – see 4 below. Type 4 first as shown, then again reversing double and single quotation marks.

4 **Drafting abbreviations** (used for speed)
These should always be typed in full. Read 5 below before starting to type it. (sep. = separate, & = and, shd. = should, rec. = receive, Dec. = December)

● 1 **Warm-up drill**
   (' ? @)

Didn't you know? Mary's Store has Conrad's cornflakes @ 75p a packet. Isn't that good value?

● 2 **Practise** [/]

The references of the lost letters are AG/md/154 and DPL/89.
Use of I/We, my/our etc in forms simplifies filling them in.
Write/phone at once for our new, bumper catalogue in colour.

● 3 **Practise** [&]

Mr & Mrs J Williams manage the new firm, Williams & Freeman.
P & O stands for Pacific & Orient, the famous shipping firm.
Shaw & Brown use an R & D team for research and development.

● 4 **Practise** ["]

"Next year," Mr Lee said, "we shall move to the new office."
"Are you sure?" he asked. "Yes" I said, "I double-checked."
"Vi was always the 'prima donna' of her class," Bob replied.

● 5 **Copy line by line**
   (abbrevs in full)

I am returning the goods under sep. cover & shd. be glad to rec. suitable replacements by the end of Dec. at the latest. If this is not possible, please return my cheque without delay.

● 6 **Test**

S1 1.04

A/S 12 (1 minute)

Thank you for your letter in which you asked us to send more chairs. We will see they reach you by the end of next week.

| | 1| | 2| | 3| | 4| | 5| | 6| | 7| | 8| | 9| | 10| | 11| | 12|

- 1 **Warm-up drill**
  (shift lock/
  hyphen/colon)

HAPPY-GO-LUCKY: UP-TO-DATE FASHIONS: GROUND-TO-AIR MISSILES:
AT-A-GLANCE AIDS: FLY-BY-NIGHT: NEVER-TO-BE-FORGOTTEN CLIMB:

- 2 **Type an A6 correspondence card for the following:**

To: Mrs A Wakeman, 33 Park Hill, ABERDEEN AB2 6BS
From Hall Appliances Ltd, 28 Market St, Aberdeen AB6 3AH
Telephone: 0224 6187

We ack with thanks yr letter of yesterday's date, wh is
receiving attention. [We will write to you asap.

- 3 **Use an A6 card.**

From The Public Library, West Parade, BRIGHTON BN2 3QP
                                        Tel. 0273 508619

Our records show that you hold 3 books wh are more
than a month overdue for return to this library.||Please
give this matter yr immed attention.

Send to: Mr A Lesley-Smith, 44 Devon Gdns,
Preston Park, Brighton BN2 4MS.

- 4 **Use an A6 card.**

Card to: Mr G Gordon, Cherry Tree Cottage, Bridford,
Exeter, Devon EX6 3AQ
Ref LT/Ford 206

We now hv 3 used cars of the make & yr you
specified. Two of them are within yr price range
& mileage limit.
We shd be pleased to arrange for you to test
drive any of these cars.

From Western Motors, 20-22 Park Rd, Exeter
Devon EX8 3GK Telephone: 0392 7684

1 **Money expressions within text**
  a Pounds and pence figures are separated by the decimal point (a full stop) – which is always followed by two figures to avoid confusion in sums like £9.50 and £9.05.
  b The £ symbol and p for pence are never both included in a single amount.
  c Amounts of pounds only can stand on their own without a decimal point followed by two zeros (see 2 below) but be consistent within a document.
  d Amounts of pence only can use pence or p (20 pence or 20p).

  The above points apply also to **dollars and cents** ($ and ¢). If your machine has no dollar and cents keys, type an oblique sign through capital S and small c respectively. Type 2 below as shown, then again with dollars and cents instead of pounds and pence.

2 **Exclamation mark**
  Many keyboards have a special key, otherwise type an apostrophe, backspace and type a full stop. The exclamation mark is followed by two spaces when it has the force of a full stop.

3 **Amendments (changes) to text** are always easy to interpret. The following are shown in 5 below.

  a **Deletions** are clearly crossed through to show the wording has been cancelled.
  b **Balloon with arrow**. The 'balloon' contains the added text, and the arrow clearly marks where it should be inserted.

● 1 **Warm-up drill**
   (/ & ")

"No," Alan replied. "Each student must sign his/her own claim. Peck & Day, the solicitors, insist on this."

● 2 **Practise £**

Amy bought a chair priced £76.50 and a table marked £123.40.

It cost me 45p more than I thought. It was £6.50 not £6.05.

The flat costs £40,000 but we can't raise more than £35,000.

● 3 **Practise !**

Look out! Stand back! Beware of the dog! Mind the ladder!

Oh no! How clever! Come on! Oh do go away! Quick - hide!

Silence! Really! Nonsense! Listen! That's right! Hello!

● 4 **Practise ( )**

The abbreviations (which represent both singular and plural) for some common metric measurements are (in brackets): metre (m), kilometre (km), centimetre (cm), millimetre (mm), gram (g), and kilogram (kg).

● 5 **Copy line by line**

Typing from manuscript makes you realise the importance of good handwriting. Most people ~~do~~ can write clearly if they take a little trouble; and when drafting for typing they must write clearly – if the typist is to make any sense of it! In ~~all~~ manuscript work spelling, too, is important for difficult and uncommon words may not always be fully legible. Use a dictionary if at all in doubt. *(at all)*

● 6 **Test**

SI 1.11

A/S 13 (1 minute)

As you type, keep your eyes on your book as much as you can. Do not get into the bad habit of watching your keys or work.

| 1| 2| 3| 4| 5| 6| 7| 8| 9| 10| 11| 12|

Cards

1 **Cards** are used in correspondence, in indexing (and other record-keeping) – and for a wide variety of purposes.

2 A6 size cards (half A5 size) are widely used, with margins not less than ½" (12 mm).

3 When typing near the bottom of a card, the lines tend to 'run off the straight'. Use of a backing sheet helps to prevent this.

4 *Correspondence cards* are used for messages which are short and not private in content.

   a One side of the card is used for the message, the other for the name and address (envelope typing guidelines apply).
   b Businesses often have their name and address printed on the message side, in one line across the top. *If typed*, this should start at the left margin, on the 4th line from the top of the card, extending to a second line if necessary. Then turn up half a line space and type a line of underscore from margin to margin (illustrated below).
   c There is no inside address, salutation, or complimentary close on correspondence cards.

● 1 **Warm-up drill**
      (concentration)

phonologically phonoasthenia phonautographically phonometers
photo phosphorus phosphorescence phosphorism phosphorylation

● 2 **Type the following on an A6 card. Address it to Mr J Adams, 24 Acacia Avenue, Norwich NR3 4SP. Follow the guidelines given above.**

BELL & LOWE, Motor Engineers, 8 Market Street
NORWICH NR6 4AJ Telephone: 0733 6128
_____

15 June 19--
Ref ST.1247

                              car
The repairs to your/have now been completed, and
it is ready to be collected. ✓We shall be open until
6.30 pm every evening this week.

The total bill amounts to £326.75 as per our telephone conversation.

---

1 **Shift lock**
This is the key above the left shift key. It is used to type consecutive capital letters and other shift key characters, and is released by pressing either left or right shift key.

2 **Underscore (shift key character)**
a Many electronic machines have an automatic underscore facility.
b To underline a short word, backspace once for each letter before underscoring.
c To underline a long word or consecutive words, rapidly move back to the starting point and engage the shift lock before underscoring (repeat action). Be careful not to overshoot the point required.
d Do not underline a final punctuation mark.

3 **Amendments to text** (4 below)
a ⊘ in the margin means 'leave as it was'. The writer changed his/her mind, so type the crossed through word(s) with a broken line underneath.
b ⌐ or // in the text means begin a new paragraph at the point indicated.
c ⌐___⌐ in the text means reverse the order

4 **Drafting abbreviations** (to be typed in full)
wl. = will, w. = with.

● 1 **Warm-up drill**
(£ () !)

I've found £20 I didn't know I had! I'll give little Annie £5.50 (for toys) and put the other £14.50 towards a good night out!

● 2 **Practise shift lock**

My mother reads the DAILY MAIL, my father prefers THE TIMES. UNESCO and UNICEF are familiar examples of UN organizations. All examination entries MUST be in BY THE END OF NEXT MONTH.

● 3 **Practise underscore**

Please come today, not next Sunday. This is most important. New classes in Word Processing are on Mondays and Thursdays. The committee meeting will start at 6.30 pm instead of 7.30.

● 4 **Copy line by line**

A typewriter is an expensive as well as a useful piece of equipment . You can both lengthen its life & produce better quality work by looking after it properly & carefully. Dust is perhaps the greatest enemy of the typewriter so keep it as clean as possible . It wl. help if you always cover the typewriter at the end of the day & whenever it wl. not be used for a period of time . Also, regularly remove the front cover of the frame & carefully brush the dust from all the accessible parts of the machine w. a long-handled, soft-bristled brush.

SI 1.16

● 5 **Test**

A/S 14 (1 minute)

We shall send you a cheque for the china just as soon as you replace the broken plates that we returned to you last week.

| | 1| | 2| | 3| | 4| | 5| | 6| | 7| | 8| | 9| | 10| | 11| | 12|

Eastbourne Language College ← (caps)
27-30 Carlyle Rd
Eastbourne
E Sussex BN24 8JX

Type on plain A4 — indented paras & shoulder headings please. Double spacing

(Principle): T Watson MA

☑ The East— L—— C—— was established in 1959 to meet the
growing ~~demand~~ ~~need~~ for courses in English as a Foreign Language
for
~~from~~ students from overseas . Courses are offered at all levels
from beginners to advanced courses for teachers & other groups
w special needs . In addition the College offers the Teacher's
Certificate course in Eng as a Foreign Language .

~~Arcom~~ Accom is arranged by the Hospitality Department .
Students are (recomended) to stay w an English family .
~~Th~~ Single or double rooms (is) available . If preferred, however,
hotel bookings may be arranged, or for longer stays a ~~private~~
flat or house can be rented .
This way they wl have considerable opp to (practice) the
language & wl make faster progress .

Facilities The college is fully equipped w audio/visual equipment .
language
There is a ⌃laboratory which is used for intensive courses . ~~to~~ Classes
are small, w a maximum of 15 students . There is a cafeteria
which serves [hot drinks & snacks] . Breakfast & the main meal
are taken w the family or at the hotel .

Excursions A full programme of excursions is available .
Visits to many well-known centres are arranged . There are
☑ ~~different~~ ~~several~~ tours of London, & tours of Windsor, Hampton Court,
Brighton, & Bath . There is a full weekend in Stratford-on-Avon .
Theatre visits can be booked . The Travel Bureau is located in
the Entrance Hall of the College .

1 **Measurements abbreviated**
   a There is no s in the plural form (1 kg, 6 kg, 1 mm, 10 mm).
   b Single and double quotation marks can be used with figures as
      abbreviations for feet and inches, with *no space* between the number
      and abbreviation (4′ 10″). (And remember, there is *no space* between
      the number and p for pence (65p).)
   c With all other abbreviations, leave *one space* between the number and
      abbreviation (4 ft, 10 in, 8 cm, 16 km).
   d Small letter x, with one space before and after it, can be used for 'by'
      (16 m x 20 m).
   e Copy small and capital letters accurately. Some abbreviations require
      capitals (eg C for Celsius, J for joule, W for watt).

2 **Amendments to text**
   a *Omit and replace*   The cancelled matter is clearly crossed through to
      show it should be omitted. The replacement text is *either* written
      above the cancelled matter *or* written within a balloon with an arrow
      to the point where it should be inserted (both included in 3 below).
   b *An unclear word* is written in capitals in the margin within an
      unbroken or broken ring. It should not of course be typed in capitals.

● 1 **Warm-up drill**
    (shift lock, u/score)

In TYPESCRIPT, words are emphasized by <u>underscoring</u>
or by the use of **bold type**. In PRINT, emphasis is shown
by the use of <u>italics</u>.

● 2 **Copy the following.**

The Chinese carpet measured 4 m x 3 m, and fitted perfectly.

Jim's brother is 6' 6" (2 m) tall and weighs 196 lb (89 kg).

The Oriental box measures precisely 165 mm x 120 mm x 80 mm.

You can express length as 25 mm (1") and 1 m (approx 3' 3").

We bought 2 kg of apples for 95p, and 2 kg of pears for 90p!

Peter drove 400 km the first day, and 350 km the second day.

The upstairs room is 12 ft 6 in x 10 ft 10 in and 7 ft high.

● 3 **Copy line by line**

(even by Harris standards.)

This strong, attractive 4-drawer filing cabinet is a real
gem of an offer, ~~by any standards we know~~. It's finished in
(OYSTER) 2-tone grey, or brown & oyster — & available only from
Harris. It's our best-selling cabinet, & ~~it~~ is fitted w.
the ~~newest~~ *latest* anti-tilt device & a 5-lever lock w. 2 keys.
And it's yours for a mere £90!

● 4 **Test**

SI 1.22

AS 15 (1 minute)

You must always think hard when you are typing and make sure
you use the right finger. Copy each word with extreme care.

| 1| 2| 3| 4| 5| 6| 7| 8| 9| 10| 11| 12|

(Type on plain A4)

OFFICE
BARCLAYS SYSTEM/FURNITURE

The hi-tech office is here with a series of ~~strong~~ ingenious units
& accessories that will adapt to all yr changing office needs.
Each unit can stand alone, or be connected to other units to
form workstation configurations.

(strong though flexible)

FOR ALL THESE REASONS YOU CAN'T BEAT BARCLAYS:

(including computer & printer table)

* 1. Strong, handsome desk units and connector tops/for any layout
or configuration.
* 2. Superb built-in wire management system copes with keyboard/VDU,
telephone, and power cables.
* 3. Every pedestal has a deep pen-tray drawer with 9 compartments
& either a deep filing drawer or two further drawers.
* 4. You can add units & components whenever you need them because
we'll be stocking them for years.

* 5. The SDR5 is ~~the~~ a world best-selling Secretarial ~~Desk~~ &
Return. The desk pedestal has deep filing drawer & 2 further
drawers. Return unit has 2 further drawers. Modesty panel
included.

* Leasing from under £3 a week
illustrated brochure
For ~~full details & illus~~ with full details, return NOW the slip
below. We will respond by return of post.

To: Barclays System Office Furniture (S486), 86-88 Derby Rd, Nottingham
NG8 4BS

Name _____
Company _____
Position _____
Address _____
_____ Postcode_____

1 **Temperature** The metric unit of temperature is degree Celsius (°C).

  a Many electronic machines have a special key for the small raised circle used. Otherwise use small letter o raised half a space (one 'click' turning a cylinder knob).
  b It is usual to leave a space after the figure in 20 °C, 15 °C etc, but not in 20°, 15°, etc.

2 **Fractions** are included on typewriter keyboards, some having more fraction keys than others.

  a Always use the key where possible.
  b When the fractions needed are not included on your keyboard, they must be made up from the figures.
  c Using the oblique sign, made-up fractions are known as sloping fractions, eg 3/10, 13/16, etc. Leave one space between a whole number and a sloping fraction, eg 4 3/10, 4 13/16, etc.

3 **Amendments to text** ⊃ in the text means do not start a new paragraph. Run on with the previous one (included in 3 below).

● 1 **Warm-up drill**
  (whole alphabet)

The flags waved gaily in the June breeze as the King and Queen's coach appeared exactly on time.

● 2 **Copy the following line by line**

  a Greater use of the metric system has led us to move from the Fahrenheit to the Centigrade (Celsius) scale for expressing temperature. The freezing point and the boiling point of water are easier to remember at 0 °C and 100 °C than 32 °F and 212 °F. The normal temperature of the human body is now expressed as 36.9 °C rather than 98.4 °F.

  b Both windows are 45 5/8 inches high and 36 7/8 inches wide. There is a 28½ inch width of wall between them.

  c The fraction can be expressed as 5 2/5 or 5.40 in decimal terms.

● 3 **Copy the following line by line.** (No space between figures and per cent symbol)

We give you 10 days to make sure you're 100% satisfied w. our equipment. In the unlikely event that you're not happy, we'll be glad to exchange it (& even collect it). That's surely fair? All we ask is to be notified within 10 days of delivery, & that the items are in good condition, as sent. So you can order direct from this cat. knowing that your satisfaction is absolutely guaranteed.

● 4 **Test**

SI 1.26

A/S 16 (1 minute)

I intend this year to learn to play bridge. My friends tell me there is no better game for pleasure and memory training.

| 1 | 2 | 3 | 4 | 5 | 6 | 7 | 8 | 9 | 10 | 11 | 12 |

UNIT 25   Temperature Fractions Amendments to text   **33**

Type on top half of plain A4 (top margin 1")
Lower half wl be used for
Illustrations & additional wording yet to be decided.

APEX INTERNATIONAL TRAVEL

The following places of interest in London will be (visit) in the course of the 2 conducted tours.

Westminster (Abby)   Hyde Park

Tower of London   Nelson Monument

Buckingham Palace   Imperial War Museum

National Gallery   British Museum

Tate Gallery   Houses of Parliament

Kensington Gdns   (St Pauls') Cathedral

Science Museum   Hampstead Heath

Natural History Museum

Regent's Park Zoo

Typist - please type in 2 columns in alphabetical order 1½ or double spacing

A4 paper and rule up

WESTFLEET PUBLICATIONS LIMITED

Major Sales Increases

this year   last year

	19--	19--	%Increase
Bradley & Scott *	42,860	29,760	44.0
Longfields	35,780	28,460	25.7
Grant & Saunders	32,650	26,380	23.8
Walters, Collingwood & Hamilton	31,430	25,160	24.9
West Bros	29,740	25,980	14.5
Faircloughs	27,850	24,640	13.0
East Midlands Publishers and Book Distributors	27,230	25,180	8.1

* Bradley & Scott extended their premises at the end of last year.

Correcting errors

From now on *as soon as you realise you have made a mistake*, correct it before going on. This is simple with electronics with a display panel where you can spot errors and correct them before the text is committed to paper or memory. On other typewriters effective correction can take time and patience. Corrections should be scarcely visible.

It is much easier to correct work while still in the typewriter. So make a habit of carefully checking each typewritten page before removing it from the machine. Use the most effective correction method for your machine.

1 **Correction paper/film strips** (available in various shades to match the paper). The error is typed again through the strip so it is covered up with the coating. The strip is then removed and the correction typed in. The same spot on the strip should not be used more than once or the error will not be covered. This method is satisfactory if the typewriter ribbon is not too dark. But if the typescript is frequently handled or folded, the coating tends to wear off, revealing the error and appearance of an overtype.

2 **Cover-up correction ribbon** – works like correction paper.

3 **Correction fluid** is sparingly applied with a small brush attached to the stopper of the bottle. Tints are available as well as standard white, to match the paper. In time the fluid thickens – and special thinner must be added.

   The error is painted out and the correction typed in *after the fluid has completely dried*: otherwise a smudge will result. Also wet fluid will smear the typewriter and ribbon. **Ensure that fluid is not spilt into the typewriter.**

4 **Rubber**
   a Lift the paper bail away.
   b Turn up the paper so the error is accessible.
   c Erase the error using a gentle up-and-down motion, blowing away the rubber dust as you do so.
   d Turn the paper back and type in the correction.

   Ensure that rubber dust does not fall into the typewriter.

5 **Lift-off correction ribbon** (electronic machines) – works only with correctable film ribbon.

● 1 **Warm-up drill**   a1 s2 d3 f4 f5 j6 j7 k8 l9 ;0 a1 s2 d3 f4 f5 j6 j7 k8 l9 ;0
    (figures)

● 2 **Copy each following sentence as given * Then make the required changes.**

John had never felt so happy in his life. (change 'John' to 'Jane', and 'his' to 'her')

I do not know when this college starts. (change 'this' to 'that', and 'starts' to 'opens')

Our present accounts show a very good profit. (change 'present' to 'current', and 'profit' to 'result')

Even with falling costs, sales were a record. (change 'falling costs' to 'reduced staff')

The Society's next social is on Friday. (change 'Society's' to 'Company's', and 'Friday' to 'Tuesday')

The warm summer helped our clothing business. (change 'warm' to 'cold', and 'clothing' to 'footwear')

● 3 **Repeat the above task until you can correct errors confidently – so they are scarcely visible.**
    Adopt this standard in all future work.

SI 1.28

● 4 **A/S 17** (1 minute)

They are very pleased with all your goods and services since they started dealing with you fifteen months ago. I am sure you will prosper in this town.

| | 1| | 2| | 3| | 4| | 5| | 6| | 7| | 8| | 9| | 10| | 11| | 12|

WP Assignment 6. *Key-in* document (MEMO) for 12-pitch print-out. Subject heading and numbered shoulder headings in bold (use automatic numbering function if available). *Text-edit* Paragraph 1 line 3: replace 'personally' with 'recently'. Transpose 1 and 2 by moving 2 as a block above 1 (cut-and-paste): change figures accordingly. *Proof-read* text on screen, and correct. *Print-out* 2 copies in 12-pitch.

From Company Secretary

To Managing Director

(Use printed memo-head)

ANNUAL CONFERENCE   Ref AST/mpo

As you asked, I hv looked into the question of suitable hotels in London for our annual conference. I wd suggest one of the following — all of which I have personally *(visited)* ~~knowledge~~. Since we must make a firm booking in the near future, it wd be helpful to have a *(word together)* chat soon.

(Please type in the numerical order shown — and inset marginal number)

④ Park Castle
   A first-class hotel in Mayfair. Excellent conference facilities. Expensive.

③ Caledonian
   A large new hotel in Bloomsbury. Gd facilities & closer to the City. Moderate charges.

① Westway
   A small, quiet hotel near Regent's Park. Facilities adequate. Restaurant excellent. Charges very reasonable.

② Commodore
   A comfortable, efficiently-run hotel in Knightsbridge. In no way outstanding, but in every way adequate.

   I hv listed the hotels in order of my preference.

Mr C Parker, 36 Ship Street, SUNDERLAND SR5 4BX   *(2 carbons & envelope please)*

Dr Mr P

Thank you for yr letter accepting our estimate for redecorating yr hall, staircase & landing. I note that you will supply the necessary quantity of wallpaper. This work will be carried out within the next 6 weeks, as you request. Just as soon as I can give a firm date for commencement of the work I will telephone you.

Yrs scly.

P Bradley
Works Manager

(Please confirm that you want all woodwork & ceilings in white.)

1 **Half-space correction** is a useful method to use in completed typescript where the error is one character more or one character less than what is required – eg 'many' for 'few' or vice versa. Most electric and electronic typewriters have a half-space correction key, which makes such substitutions simple. (This correction method is also known as 'stretching' and 'squeezing').

2 After half-space correction, the *spacing* before and after the word is slightly different from standard spacing. However, it is an acceptable alternative to retyping the page, and if well done is not penalised in exams.

3 **On manual typewriters** (after blanking out or erasing the incorrect word):

a *Add one character* (eg correcting 'few' to 'many') by skilful use of the backspace key (pressing it half-way down moves the printing point back only half a space). The space before and after the corrected word will then be half a character space instead of a full one.

b *Reduce by one character* (eg correcting 'many' to 'few') by skilful use of the space bar. When the space bar is pressed down *and held down*, the printing point has moved forward only half a space: releasing the space bar allows it to move forward the other half space. The space before and after the corrected word will then be one and a half character spaces instead of the usual one.

4 **Amendments to text**
a An instruction to the typist is written within a balloon to keep it clearly apart from the text (included in 3 below).
b Striking through capital letters means change to small letters.

• 1 **Warm-up drill**
(whole alphabet)

A keen and exciting quiz game was played on television by housewives from Jersey.

• 2 **Copy each sentence as it stands * Then remove the incorrect word and make the substitution given * Repeat each sentence until you can make the half-space correction well and without hesitation.**

We sent it in May with the invoice. (correct 'May' to 'June')

I cannot find this books. (correct 'this' to 'those')

Your check did not arrive. (correct 'check' to 'cheque')

It contains many mistakes. (correct 'many' to 'few')

We gave it to them yesterday. (correct 'them' to 'him')

I arrived at four o'clock.   (correct 'four' to 'one')

• 3 **Copy line by line.**

(Typist – double spacing please)

This Booklet tells Investors new to the Stock Market how to buy & sell Shares. It includes a Check List of questions which all would-be shareholders shd ask themselves. First & foremost is whether they are prepared to see the value of their Investment fall, perhaps steeply. In good times it is easy to forget that Shares go down as well as up.

SI 1.17

• 4 **A/S 18** (1 minute)

Take care to sit well when you type. Keep both your feet on the floor, one slightly in front of the other. See that you are relaxed, to avoid fatigue.

| 1 | 2 | 3 | 4 | 5 | 6 | 7 | 8 | 9 | 10 | 11 | 12 |

- 1 **Warm-up drill**
  (spaced caps)

- 2 **Present the following information in the form of a ruled table as shown in the example * use A5 portrait paper.**

YR DAY-TIME FLIGHTS TO THE SUN
April 19-- to ~~Nov~~ Oct 19--

To FARO - Thursday flights} E Midlands 0800 hrs,
Gatwick 0700, Manchester 0715

To GERONA - Friday flights} E Midlands 0845,
Gatwick 0710, Manchester 0830

To MALAGA - Wed flights} E Midlands 1500, Gatwick 1615,
Manchester 1545

To ALICANTE - Sat flights} E M 1720, Gatwick 1630,
Manchester 1645

To PALMA - Tues flights} E M 1745, G —— 1645,
M —— 1500

UK Airport	Destination	Day	Depart UK
E Midlands	Faro	Thurs	0800
Gatwick	Faro	Thurs	0700
Manchester	Faro	Thurs	0715

- 3 **Use A4 paper and add a fifth column to the above, headed Arrive UK * extract the times for the fifth column from the information below * rule up.**

From FARO Arrive UK at 1445 (E Midlands) 1300 (Gatwick) 1330 (M)
  "   Gerona   "   "   "   1420   1150   1350
  "   Malaga   "   "   "   2100   2300   2200
  "   Alicante   "   "   "   2300   2240   2255
  "   Palma   "   "   "   2250   2150   2000

Setting margins

You will now start setting margins – left, right, and top – and decide your own line-endings instead of copying from the book line by line.

1 **A4 paper width** Hold a sheet of A4 paper against the paper scales with the left edge at 0, and note the number at the right edge, as follows:

82 pica (10 characters to 25 mm or 1"). 100 elite (12 characters to 25 mm or 1").

2 **Side margins** can thus be easily worked out. Two examples follow.

1" left and ½" right – pica at 10 and 77 – elite at 12 and 94
1" left and 1" right – pica at 10 and 72 – elite at 12 and 88

3 **Top and bottom margins** are measured by lines of type to the inch. 6 lines in single spacing (both pica and elite) measure one inch. (Confirm this by typing your name 6 times in single spacing and measuring.)

For a 1" top margin turn up 7 times in single spacing (you type on the 7th line).
For a 2" top margin turn up 13 times in single spacing – and so on.

The *bottom margin* on A4 paper should not be less than 1" – but you will not need to apply this for the present.

4 On machines with **Automatic line turn-up** facility, you do not need to decide each line ending yourself. Once margins are set, the machine automatically turns up for a new line when the next word will not fit within the right margin setting (the machine responding to the space bar). This is also known as the 'word trap' facility.

5 **Warning bleep or bell** sounds when you approach the right-hand margin setting. Find out how many characters you can type after the bleep or bell before *your* machine locks at the margin setting (electronics in Normal typing mode). Knowing this will help you judge when to turn up for a new line so that you keep your right-hand margin reasonably even and close to the margin setting *without dividing words*. (You will learn word division in Unit 39.)

6 **Margin release key** must be pressed once the machine locks – to enable you to complete the word you are typing. Aim to use this key as little as possible or it will slow down your typing.

● 1 **Warm-up drill**
(alphabet/
space bar)

a b c d e f g h i j k l m n o p q r s t u v w x y z

● 2 **Type the following in double spacing on A4 paper * Left margin 1", right margin ½", top margin 2" * Keep your right-hand margin as even as possible without dividing words.**

In the business ~~word~~ *world*, practice ~~can~~ differs on the size of margins used in typewritten work. Some prefer wide margins – which assist ease of reading and provide a pleasing frame to a document. Others think it matters more to be economical with paper, and use narrow margins – so that one sheet of paper often suffices instead of two. Often the size of margins is left to the typist's judgement and she must balance both points of view in relation to the task in hand. Many employers (and some examining bodies) advise against dividing words at the end of lines in general work. They consider it a waste of time for typists to strive too hard for an even right-hand margin. Concentration is broken and time lost each time a decision has to be made about where to divide a word. Certainly a reasonably even right margin can be achieved without word division. Nevertheless there are times when division is necessary, and guidelines for this will be given in Unit 39. For the present do not divide words at the end of lines. The only divisions you may make are hyphenated words – dividing at the permanent hyphen (hyphen at <u>end</u> of the line).

(wh. is not always a straightforward matter)

SI 1.12

● 3 **A/S 19** (1 minute)

I wrote to you before Christmas to ask if you could offer me a job as a clerk in your office. You said that I should try in June. This I am now doing.

Sub-divided columns When a column heading is *wider* than the combined columns below it (including space between columns) it is suitably divided, and typed in single spacing (illustrated below).

- **1 Warm-up drill**
  (shift keys/ concentration)

  Adelaide Berlin Capetown Dublin Exeter Faro Glasgow Harlech;
  Ipswich Jaffa Karachi Lagos Madrid Nairobi Oslo Paris Quebec
  Rome Sale Tangier Utrecht Valencia Warsaw Xenia Yalta Zurich

- **2 Use A4 paper and above guidelines * centre Country vertically with the other column headings (you need to use the half-spacer).**

EXCELSIOR MOTORS LIMITED (UK)
Comparative Export Figures for 19-- and 19-- *[last year then year before last]*

Country	Saloon and Estate Cars		Sports Cars/ Racing Cars	
	19--	19--	19--	19--
Germany	10,560	9,899	357	291
France	8,288	8,109	168	150
Holland	870	761	68*	75
Italy	780	768	65	54
Belgium	525*	583	52	48
Norway	221	186	45	40
Sweden	350	302	168	155
Denmark	324	296	88	74
United States of America	5.351	4,213	624	325
TOTAL	27,269	25,117	1,635	1,212

typist – countries in alpha order please

type in full as given

* Reduction in sales

- 1 **Warm-up drill**
  (figures)

Numbers can be divided evenly by 3 if the sum of the digits is divisible by 3 - 309, 678, 2,895, 15,786 478,674. (In these numbers the digits total 12, 21, 24, 27, 36. Check that yours are correct.) Where, as with the last 2 numbers, the sum of the digits is divisible by 9, the numbers also are divisible by 9.

- 2 **Type the following on A4 paper in double spacing with side margins of 1″ and ½″, and a top margin of 1½″ * Start the heading at the left margin, and leave 2 lines of space between the heading and the start of the text.**

Typist - indented paras please

DEVELOPING MARGIN SENSE

Unless you are given instructions for margins, you will have to choose yr own. To do this well, you need to judge the amount of text in relation to the size of paper & the line-spacing to be used. // The aim shd be for the text to appear pleasingly on the page – neither too high nor too low, & not too far to the left or right.

This is a skill that you can develop with practice. While you are still being given margin guidance, make the most of it. Each time you finish a document, carefully consider how well placed the text appears in relation to the margins & line-spacing used.

As a general rule the right margin shd not be wider than the left one (it makes the page look lop-sided). On A4 paper, margins shd not be less than one inch (25 mm) at the top, bottom, + left of the page. The right-hand margin shd not be less than half an inch. If the text is short, margins can be bigger. Equal side margins of one inch are widely used for general work. // Good presentation skill is one of the hallmarks of the expert typist.

HALLMARKS

SI 1.13

- 3 **A/S 20** (1 minute)

The school to be built next year will take boys and girls of junior school age. There will still be a lack of places for students in senior age groups.

| | 1 | 2 | 3 | 4 | 5 | 6 | 7 | 8 | 9 | 10 | 11 | 12 |

1. **Sub-divided columns** occur in some tables (shown below).

2. The upper heading starts at the tab stop for the first column below it.

3. One line of space is left between a heading and its sub-divisions.

● 1 **Warm-up drill**
(shift lock/ underscore)

Don't fail to attend our BUMPER SUMMER SALE on 20-25 August.
WILSON & MANN are premier household suppliers in AVONBRIDGE.

● 2 **A4 paper * centre Country and Capital vertically with the Population headings * rule up.**

Typist – countries in alpha order please

SOME WORLD POPULATION FIGURES[1]

Country	Capital	Population	
		Total	Capital
Egypt	Cairo	38,000,000	8,143,000
Kenya	Nairobi	12,934,000	509,000
Nigeria	Lagos	79,760,000	2,000,000
Tanzania	Dar-es-Salaam	16,031,000	623,000
Canada	Ottawa	22,993,000	693,300
USA	Washington DC	215,892,000	2,910,111
E Germany[2]	East Berlin	16,767,000	1,094,147
W Germany[3]	Bonn	61,352,700	284,000
India	Delhi	606,200,000	4,065,698
Austria	Vienna	7,519,900	1,593,000
Spain	Madrid	36,240,000	3,146,071

1 Figures are in some cases approximations or estimates
2 German Democratic Republic
3 Federal Republic of Germany (including West Berlin)

Proofreading

1 **Mailability or usability** Proofreading (and correcting errors) is a vital part of typewriting skill. In offices, typed documents *must* be error free, pleasing to look at, and all instructions followed. Only then is the work 'mailable' or 'usable'.

2 **Retype poor work** Examinations recognise the need for this very high standard and allow only a limited number of word faults and presentation faults overall for a 'pass'. Therefore if, after checking a page of typescript, you find two or more mistakes that you cannot correct neatly, or feel that the work is messy or very badly positioned on the paper, *you should type it again*. If you start this habit *now*, you are more likely to succeed in examinations and in office work.

3 **Portfolio** Keep a portfolio containing only your *error-free, well-presented work* to help develop a pride in excellence. This will be useful in other ways too – work exhibitions, continuous assessment by your teacher, job applications, etc. Note in pencil the number of attempts you had to make, and aim to reduce this progressively.

4 **Proofreading** You will already have corrected any errors you spotted while you were typing. Now you must check each page again while still in the typewriter. Turn up your typescript in the machine line by line, using the paper bail as a guide. As you find an error, correct it if possible: otherwise ring it with a pencil.

Scrutinise what you have typed, not what you *think* or *hope* you have typed. *Check word for word, figure for figure, and space for space*. You will then find errors that would not be obvious at a glance – incorrect dates, figures and names, transpositions, words or lines omitted, etc.

5 **Double check** Then exchange your work with a classmate, or get someone else to check it for you. Every error *must* be found. With the paper out of the machine, adopt the following method of checking. Place the draft and typescript alongside one another on the desk before you. With your free hand, hold a ruler under the first line of the draft to guide your eye. With a pencil in your other hand to ring errors in the typescript, scrutinise the draft and typescript alternately, word by word. Move the ruler line by line down the draft copy as you proceed.

6 **Retype or file** Finally, retype the task if it does not meet the standard outlined in 2 above. If it is free of errors, file it in your portfolio. In future, follow the above procedure for all your work.

● **1 Warm-up drill**
   (shift keys)

aA bB cC dD eE fF gG hH iI jJ kK lL mM nN oO pP qQ rR sS tT
uU vV wW xX yY zZ aA bB cC dD eE fF gG hH iI jJ kK lL mM nN

● **2 Check the typescript below, and find the five errors it contains.**

> Please look into/2 letters of complaint
> received from Hunt & Johnston
> (account No 605437). They allege
> (wrongly I think) that we failed to
> meet our delivery schedule; and
> that our packing was inferior,
> resulting in several breakages.
> They are good customers we do
> not wish to lose.

Please look into the 2 letters of com-
plaint recieved from Hunt & Johnson
(account No 604537). They allege
(wrongly I think) that we failed to
meet our delivery schedule; and that
our packing was inferior, resulting in
several breakages. They are good customers we do not wish to loose.

SI 1.20

● **3 A/S 21** (1 minute)

It is easy to recognize a skilled typist. Not only does she type fast but she also does things the right way. Watch how she sits and holds her wrists.

| 1| 2| 3| 4| 5| 6| 7| 8| 9| 10| 11| 12|

Multiple-line column headings (ruled) In ruled tables, where the number of lines in the column headings varies, they look best when centred vertically with each other, as shown below. (You need to use half-spacing for the first column heading.

• 1 **Warm-up drill**
   (fractions) $8\frac{1}{2} + 3\frac{3}{4} - 2\frac{1}{4} = 10$

• 2 **Use A5 paper * centre column headings vertically, as shown * rule up.**

MAYFLOWER LOTTERY

Christmas Draw

(Winning numbers drawn on 24 December)

Name of Winner	Ticket No	Special Christmas Prizes
		£
Mrs P Goodbody	18162	5,000
Dr E Dische	31713	3,000
Miss W Lang	23835	2,000
Mr F Berry	36560	1,000
Miss P Fortune	11749	750
Ms E Peck	24063	500
Mr M Saleem	17634	250
Mrs S Terry	20461	100

Mr T Cummings 35996 £50

Anyone with a ticket with the last
4 ~~6~~ digits the same as in the winning *top*
number should apply for a prize of
£25.

• 3 **Type again the table in Unit 116 * centre the column headings vertically * rule up the table.**

Blocked headings

1 Many documents have a general heading at the top, and perhaps sub-headings with it. The lines of the heading are usually typed in different styles for different emphasis and clarity of meaning, as follows:

B U S I N E S S   S T U D I E S   D E P A R T M E N T

PRELIMINARY ANALYSIS OF EVENING CLASS FIGURES

Session 19-- to 19--

2 **Spaced capitals** are used for the first line above (one space between letters, three spaces between words). When typing headings, always follow the style given in the draft.

3 **Bold type** is available on electronic typewriters – an additional feature for use in headings.

4 **Line spacing** leave one line of space between lines in a heading. Then leave two lines of space before starting to type the text beneath it.

5 **Blocked headings** (as shown above) at the left margin can be used whether the following text is in blocked or indented paragraphs.

● 1 **Warm-up drill**
(alphabet build up)

abc abcd abcde abcdef abcdefg abcdefgh abcdefghi abcdefghij abcdefghijk abcdefghijkl abcdefghijklm abcdefghijklmn abcdef ghijklmno abcdefghijklmnop abcdefghijklmnopq abcdefghijklmno pqr abcdefghijklmnopqrs abcdefghijklmnopqrst abcdefghijklmno pqrstu abcdefghijklmnopqrstuv abcdefghijklmnopqrstuvw abcdef ghijklmnopqrstuvwx abcdefghijklmnopqrstuvwxy abcdefghijklmno pqrstuvwxyz abc abcd abcde abcdef abcdefg abcdefgh abcdefghi

● 2 **Type a mailable copy of the following on A4 paper in double spacing * add the 3-line heading given above * Margins: left 1″, right ½″, top 2″.**

Typist – blocked paragraphs please

In September there was a greater than usual interest in evening classes for the new session. By the beginning of October, 25 classes were in operation with a minimum of 18 students per class. In all, *on the previous session* student enrolment was 13 per cent up. //Towards the end of the first term there was a gradual but steady decrease in student attendance.

At the start of the Spring Term student numbers were so depleted that classes, where possible, had to be amalgamated. In a few cases, classes had to be closed.

This situation led to serious disruption of learning for many students. At the same time, teachers were fully stretched. By the *original* end of the session only 14 out of the 25 classes were still operating. //A questionnaire is to be sent to each student who dropped out to find out the reason - to try to take steps to see that such a disastrous situation does not occur again.

SI 1.08

● 3 **A/S 22** (2 minutes)

The telephone has a big place in our lives, both at work and in the home. More and more use is made of it both for local and long-distance calls. The great thing is to be clear and brief, so that you keep down the cost and do not waste time.

| | 1| | 2| | 3| | 4| | 5| | 6| | 7| | 8| | 9| | 10| | 11| | 12|

Ruling tables

1 **Ruling tables** can assist clarity and ease of reading. Ruling is easy provided the table has been well typed, with equal space between columns.

2 Use a transparent ruler and black ball-point or fine felt-tip pen, and place your typed table over a card or several sheets of paper before ruling the lines.

3 First rule in lines lightly with a soft pencil – to ensure neat corners to the outer frame, and to check straightness. Turn the table round when ruling the vertical lines – so you are always ruling from left to right, for pen and ruler control.

a Rule in the outer frame, with equal space (approximately one character space) between the typing and the line on all four sides.

b Rule in the horizontal then vertical lines that run the full width and length of the table. Finally, any part-lines. All these lines should be approximately mid-way between type at the nearest point.

c Carefully erase any pencil marks after inking in.

With practice, it will be possible to dispense with pre-ruling in pencil except for the outer frame.

● 1 **Warm-up drill**
    (Roman numerals)

Roman numerals use 7 symbols, sometimes known as the Units and Fives. The Units are I (1), X (10), C (100), and M (1,000). The Fives are V (5), L (50), and D (500).

● 2 **Use A4 paper * rule up as shown.**

HOLIDAYS IN BRITAIN

See the Country by Coach

Some Selected Tours

Name of Tour	Days	Price	Hotels
		£	
Southern Country Houses	10	350	Hastings Southampton Exeter
The West Country	14	490	Bath Taunton Plymouth Truro
University Highlights	7	245	Oxford Cambridge
The Lake District	7	245	Keswick Kendal
Scottish Highlights	14	490	Oban Edinburgh Perth Inverness

Centred headings

1. **Centred headings** are simple on machines with an Automatic Centring facility – and therefore widely used on them. On machines without this facility, the starting position for each centred line has to be worked out as described below: since this takes time, only centre headings if you are instructed to. If you do centre, it *must* be done accurately.

2. **Centring a heading over equal margins** A heading should always be centred over the typing line. This is easier if margins are equal in width – for then the centre point of the typing line and of the paper is the same. With equal margins, proceed as follows (each line must be taken separately).

   a. Move to the centre point of the typing line, ie centre of the paper.
   b. Backspace once for each two characters (letter/spaces) in the heading, saying them to yourself in pairs as you do so.
   c. Start typing the heading at the scale point reached.

   (Explanatory diagrams are given below for pica and elite type, showing side margins of one inch.)

d **Pica type and A4 paper**

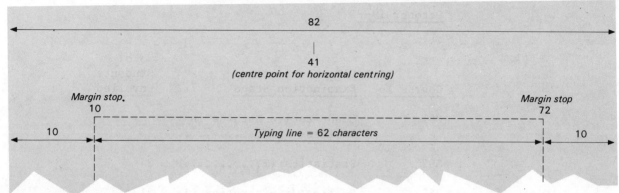

e **Elite type and A4 paper**

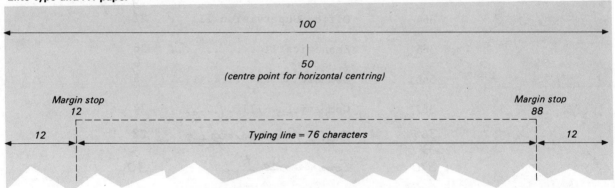

3. **Centring a heading over unequal margins** requires calculation to find the centre point of the typing line.
   a. Add together the numbers at which the margins are set, eg 15 + 77 = 92.
   b. Divide the answer by two – 92 ÷ 2 = 46.
   c. Backspace from scale point 46 once for each two characters in the heading.
   d. Start typing the heading at the scale point reached.

- 1 **Warm-up drill**
  (alphabet/comma)

  a, b, c, d, e, f, g, h, i, j, k, l, m, n, o, p, q, r, s, t,
  u, v, w, x, y, z, a, b, c, d, e, f, g, h, i, j, k, l, m, n,

- 2 On A4 paper type again task 2 in Unit 31 * centre the headings * side margins of one inch * indented paragraphs.
- 3 Repeat the task, this time with side margins of 1½″ and ½″ * blocked paragraphs.

1 Where the number of lines in the column headings varies in unruled tables, they are typed so they all line up *either* across the bottom line *or* across the top line (both styles are shown below). Always follow the style in the copy.

2 Multiple-line column headings on unruled tables are underscored – the underscore typed in a straight line across the page beneath the bottom line of type, as shown below.

- 1 **Warm-up drill**
  (figures)

  a1 s2 d3 f4 f5 j6 j7 k8 19 ;0 a1 s2 d3 f4 f5 j6 j7 k8 19 ;0

- 2 **Use A4 paper.**

  B U S I N E S S   S T U D I E S   D E P A R T M E N T

  EVENING CLASS ENROLMENTS

  October 19--

Course No	Class Subject and Examination Stage	No of Students Enrolled
361	Quantitative Methods in Business III	26
362	Statistics II	24
363	Public Administration III	21
364	Office Supervision III ..	2*8*
365	Economics II	26
366	Commercial Law II	2*6*
367	Company Law III	24
368	Data Processing I	28
370	Commerce I	30
371	" II	27
372	Accounting I	24
373	" II	27
369	Data Processing II	29

- 3 **Type the above table again, with the column headings lined up across the top line. They will appear as follows:**

Course No	Class Subject and Examination Stage	No of Students Enrolled

1 **Amendments (changes) to text.** You have already used most of the changes listed below, but they are all brought together for revision and consolidation. Reading carefully through the draft copy for meaning usually makes clear what is required. In the past, signs and symbols derived from printing were used although many drafters did not know them. The currently used methods given below have the advantage of simplicity and clarity.

a **Deletions** – clearly crossed through to show the wording has been cancelled and should be omitted.

b **Deletions with replacement** – replacement text written above *or* within a balloon with arrow to insertion point.

c **Added word(s)** – either written above where to be inserted, with a caret sign *or* within a balloon with arrow.

d **Instruction(s) to typist** – written within a balloon and kept apart from the text.

2 **Amendment signs and their meaning**

a ⌐ or ∥ means start a new paragraph at the point indicated.

b ⌐⌐ means reverse the order horizontally.

c ⌐↑ or ⌐ means reverse the order vertically.

d ⌐ means do not start a new paragraph. Run on with the previous one.

e ∧ (caret sign) means insert given matter here.

f ⊘ in the margin means retain the crossed through word(s) with the dotted line below.

g ⌒ means no space between the characters or words marked.

h Stroke between characters or words means leave a space.

i Striking through capital letter(s) means change to small letter(s).

j (caps) means change to capital letters.

k (spaced caps) means change to spaced capital letters.

---

a We are sorry that you found ~~such serious~~ fault with the raincoat we recently sent you.

b Please report the matter ~~without delay~~ *at once* to Mr Jones, the Senior Assistant in the Furniture Sales (new) Department.

c If you travel on Sunday, *and George* you should enquire in good time whether delay is to be expected. *because of repair work on the railway line,*

d Remember that the station where you will get out has been renamed Whyteleafe South. *Typist-name in caps please and spelt as here.*

a I shall reply to your kind letter in full. ∥ Meanwhile, the author you asked about is William Watts.

b He looked |drawn| pale| and indeed very ill.

c Adams, J   Adams, J
    Baxter, P   or Baxter, P
    Barnes, T   Barnes, T

d Last year's sales figures were a record.
    They will be difficult to surpass.

e Next term, swimming classes will be held in the open. *weather permitting,*

f Her exam results do not reflect her ability, ~~but she is very lazy.~~ ⊘

g They arrived be fore noon.

h The goods have still not arrived.

i Where is the nearest Police Station?

j Notes on the Accounts. ← (caps)

k AGENDA ← (spaced caps)

- 1 **Warm-up drill**   a b c d e f g h i j k l m n n o p q r s t u v w x y z
  (alphabet/space bar)

- 2 **Study the above, then type the matter in the right-hand column, making the amendments indicated.**

  SI 1.38

- 3 **A/S 23** (2 minutes)   Car production is likely to rise steadily in this country in the next few years. Thanks to greater efficiency in the use of machines as well as manpower, we can now compete with all our main rivals. If we don't relax, the prospect is bright.

  | 1| 2| 3| 4| 5| 6| 7| 8| 9| 10| 11| 12|

1 Multiple-line column headings are typed in single spacing.

2 A long item in the first column (the descriptive column) should be divided, and typed in single spacing. Leader dots are then typed only on the last line.

● **1 Warm-up drill**
 (alphabet/
 space bar)

a b c d e f g h i j k l m n o p q r s t u v w x y z

● **2 Use A4 paper.**

EXPENDITURE ESTIMATES

Recreation and Community Activities

	19--/-- Original Estimate	19--/-- Revised Estimate
	£	£
Playing Fields	86,250	90,000
Tennis Courts	10,160	11,200
Swimming Baths[1]	74,360	48,750
Play Centres	8,555	9,115
Community Centres[2]	75,346	77,890
Other Community Activities and Facilities	8,000	8,500
TOTAL	£262,671	£245,455

forthcoming year

1 The building of the proposed new swimming pool in the Downland Community Centre has been postponed indefinitely.

2 Including Senior Citizens Club.

1 **Drafting abbreviations** To save time when handwriting a draft that is to be typed, many people use abbreviations. Examples are *&* (and), shd (should), wd (would), recd (received) and Yrs ffly (Yours faithfully). Many others occur, some in fairly common use but others simply an individual's choice.

Some writers of drafts generally follow drafting abbreviations with a full stop to make clear that they are abbreviations. Others do not use full stops. Yet others are inconsistent in their use of stops. The vital thing is that you *identify the correct word for typing in full, and spell it correctly.* As you know, before you can identify the correct words you should carefully read through the manuscript draft for meaning. Sometimes an unclear word or abbreviation becomes clear when read in context or when you become more familiar with the writing.

2 **Drafting abbreviations used in RSA Stage 1 typewriting examinations**

accommodation	*accom .*	immediately	*immed .*	shall	*sh .*
account(s)	*a/c (s)*	inconvenient/ence	*incon .*	should	*shd .*
acknowledge	*ack .*	manufacturer(s)	*mfr(s) .*	which	*wh .*
advertisement(s)	*advert (s) .*	miscellaneous	*misc .*	would	*wd .*
appointment(s)	*appt (s) .*	necessary	*necy .*	with	*w .*
approximately	*approx .*	opportunity/ies	*opp (s) .*	will	*wl .*
believe	*bel .*	receipt(s)	*rec (s) .*	year(s)	*yr (s) .*
business	*bus .*	receive	*rec .*	your(s)	*yr (s) .*
catalogue(s)	*cat (s) .*	received	*recd .*	dear	*dr .*
committee(s)	*cttee (s) .*	recommend	*recom .*		
company/ies	*co (s) .*	reference(s)	*ref (s) .*	days of the week	
definitely	*def .*	referred	*refd .*	eg *Thurs. Fri .*	
develop	*dev .*	responsible	*resp .*	months of the year	
exercise	*ex .*	secretary/ies	*sec (s) .*	eg *Jan . Feb .*	
expense(s)	*exp (s) .*	separate	*sep .*	words in addresses	
experience	*exp .*	signature(s)	*sig (s) .*	eg *Rd . Cres .*	
government(s)	*gov (s) .*	sufficient	*suff .*	complimentary	
guarantee(s)	*gntee (s) .*	temporary	*temp .*	closes	
		through	*thro`*	eg *ffly .*	

3 **Additional drafting abbreviations** Other examining bodies, and drafters in offices, may use different and additional abbreviations to the ones listed above. However, these should present no problem *when carefully considered in context.*

4 **Abbreviations to be retained in typescript** Widely used Latin abbreviations such as ie, etc, eg, viz, should always be typed in their abbreviated form as this is correct usage. In addition, you should not alter abbreviations used in names such as Mr, Mrs, Esq, Col, D & R Motors, etc.

5 **Spelling** Typing from manuscript requires close attention to spelling. If you are in any doubt about a word, consult a dictionary – which should always be to hand when you type. It is a good idea to keep a *Vocabulary Notebook,* listing alphabetically all words new to you (with their meaning) and words you tend to mis-spell.

- 1 **Warm-up drill**
  (figures)   a1 s2 d3 f4 f5 j6 j7 k8 l9 ;0 a1 s2 d3 f4 f5 j6 j7 k8 l9 ;0

- 2 **Copy on A4 paper (with a 1″ left and top margin) the list of words in (2) above * use heading WORDS OFTEN ABBREVIATED IN MS DRAFTS * type the words in one column down the page, each word starting at the left margin * remove paper from machine and rule a vertical line down the page just to the right of the longest typed word * then write in alongside the appropriate drafting abbreviation for each word * learn the spelling of all the words.**

- 3 **Fold back the paper along your ruled line to obscure the words * reinsert paper into machine * alongside each abbreviation, type the word it represents * carefully check all spellings.**

Tabulation

1 An **itinerary** is a summary of travel arrangements, appointments, etc, on a business trip.

2 For clarity, a column arrangement is generally used – so tab stops should be set. Itineraries are thus a form of tabulation.

3 A carbon copy is usually taken for office reference.

• 1 **Warm-up drill** *(double letters)*

```
kraal, rubber, acclaim, ladder, deed, suffer, egg, fill,
hammer, sinner, soon, upper, arrest, kiss, mutter, buzz,
Sally-Anne Summers looked in terror at the compass needle.
```

• 2 **Use A4 paper * take two carbon copies.**

CHAIRMAN'S VISIT TO HOLLAND
16 and 17 September 19--

(Accompanied by Mr WG Williams)

16 September (Tuesday)	1500 hrs	Depart Head Office by car
	1600 hrs	Arrive Heathrow Airport for check-in
	1650 hrs	Depart Heathrow
	1740 hrs	Arrive Amsterdam (Schiphol)
		Met by Mr Van Lennep & driven to Ritz Hotel, Dam Place (LENNEP)
	1930 hrs	Dinner at Ritz with Dutch Exporters
		Overnight at Ritz Hotel
17 September (Wednesday)	1000 hrs	Meeting at Ritz with Dutch agents
	1250 hrs	Car at Ritz Hotel
	1300 hrs	Luncheon at Den Haag Restaurant with Amsterdam Chamber of Commerce
	→ 1800 hrs car at Ritz Hotel	
	1815 hrs	Check-in at Schiphol Airport
	1850 hrs	Depart " "
	1940 hrs	Arrive Heathrow

Documents — Latest Balance Sheet
Details of last 2 years' sales to Holland
Luncheon & Dinner Guest Lists

- 1 **Warm-up drill**
  (phrases)

on the, in the, to the, from the, and the, if the, when the, is the, at the, with the, and we shall, if they will, it is, when do you, how can he, what do you, thank you for, we hope

- 2 A4 paper * side margins 1″ and ½″ * top margin 2″.

Success in Typing ← *(all in caps)*

(Typist – use double spacing please)

Need for Good Standard of English

Success in typing requires a good knowledge of English. Documents have to be produced from drafts — often in manuscript that is by no means ~~legible~~ + easy to read.

(all unclear) Careful + intelligent reading of the draft is necy. if words + all abbreviations are to be correctly identified + typed, + ^any amendments to the text ~~correctly~~ made. ✓ As part of yr general training, read carefully at all times. Note constantly ~~noting~~ the use of words + punctuation, + the construction of sentences + paragraphs. Careful reading, always using a dictionary when in doubt, is the best way to improve [vocabulary + spelling].

In the world of work it is the responsibility of the typist to ensure that the documents ~~she~~ produced are error free and well presented. If they are not, they are value less. Therefore never leave one task + proceed to another until you are satisfied it is 'mailable'. That way you will save time in the end.

22 October 19 ——
JKM/BAS

SI 1.19

- 3 **A/S 24** (2 minutes)

A good secretary should have a feel and a love for language. For this it helps just to read a lot of good books. Writing of any sort trains the mind to choose apt words and phrases. A good style grows with practice, and brings its own reward.

| 1   2   3   4   5   6   7   8   9   10   11   12 |

A zither is a musical instrument with metal strings fixed over a flat wooden frame which rests on a table or just on the player's knees. It should not be confused with the sitar, an Indian instrument quite like a long-necked guitar.

• 2 **Use A4 paper to type the 2-column questionnaire.**

INDUSTRIAL RELATIONS

Question   Answer

(1) Give THREE grounds on which an   (a) ....
    employer may dismiss an   (b) ....
    employee fairly.   (c) ....

(2) Which Government-sponsored
    organization was set up in 1975
    to assist in resolving industrial
    disputes?   ....

(3) Which of the following advantages   CHEAPER
    has an Industrial Tribunal got   LEGAL REPRESENTATION
    over a court of law? (Delete as   UNNECESSARY
    appropriate)   HEARS HEARSAY EVIDENCE ALLOWED

(4) You can be fairly dismissed for
    going on strike.   TRUE/FALSE? ....

(5) What do the letters ACAS stand for?   ....

(6) You can claim unfair dismissal
    if you were dismissed for a fair
    reason but were not allowed to
    present your/defence. (own)   TRUE/FALSE? ....

(7) What THREE remedies can an   (a) ....
    Industrial Tribunal offer to   (b) ....
    an employee who has been   (c) ....
    dismissed unfairly?

(8) The right to appeal to an
    Industrial Tribunal for unfair
    dismissal does not apply to
    employees of firms with fewer
    than 20 employees.   TRUE/FALSE? ....

Paragraph headings

1 A **paragraph heading** is typed on the same line as the start of the paragraph.

2 Leave 2 spaces (consistently) between the paragraph heading and the start of the paragraph – which may be typed in single, 1½, or double spacing.

3 Paragraph headings may be in capital letters (without underscoring); with initial capitals (underscored); or in bold type. Follow the style given in the copy.

4 Sometimes paragraph headings are followed by a full stop or a colon (consistently). Again, follow the copy.

5 Leave at least one line of space (consistently) between the paragraphs.

● 1 **Warm-up drill**
(*figures*)

We have noted your change of address from 247 High Street to 398 Park Avenue. The 5 copies of our 60-page catalogue will be sent to you before 1 May. I must remind you that we have not yet received your cheque for £456.87 to cover our Invoice number G23901. This order for 4 tables and 24 chairs was despatched to you on 5 March on the understanding that payment would be made within 30 days.

● 2 **A4 paper * side margins 1″ * top margin 1½″**

MAKING THE BEST USE OF THE POST

Double spacing please

ORDINARY LETTER POST AND PARCEL POST: These services meet most normal needs. Every day ~~in Britain~~ millions of letters and parcels are sent by ordinary post - and the vast majority arrive safely.

REGISTERED POST: This provides special security for letters and packets, and compensation for damage or loss. It is the best way to send ~~small amounts of~~ cash and small articles of value. However, compensation for cash will not be paid unless it is sent in one of the registered letter envelopes sold by the Post Office.

RECORDED DELIVERY: Where the important thing is to have a record of posting and delivery rather than compensation for loss, letters and packets may be sent by recorded delivery. This is cheaper than registered post.

The sender is handed a date-stamped and initialled certificate of posting at the post office: and the recipient signs on delivery to provide a record of receipt.

COMPENSATION FEE PARCEL SERVICE: This is intended for larger articles of value, for which compensation is desired in the event of loss or damage. Unlike registered letters, these parcels receive no special security handling in the post to reduce the risk of loss or damage: the benefit is in the right to compensation should such occur. A certificate is given as evidence of posting.

● 3 **Type task 2 again * single spacing * paragraph headings with initial capitals and underscored * no colon at end of paragraph headings * top margin 2″.**

SI 1.37

● 4 **A/S 25** (2 minutes)

More and more people are using bicycles to get themselves to work, to do their shopping - or merely to ride for pleasure. This results from many factors, the most important being the high cost of transport, and the real need for more exercise.

| 1 | 2 | 3 | 4 | 5 | 6 | 7 | 8 | 9 | 10 | 11 | 12 |

- **1** **Warm-up drill**
  (suffixes)

  usable durable notable eatable mailable breakable noticeable
  leakage outrage wastage frontage pilotage roughage shortages

- **2** **Fill in the top copy of the A4 form you typed in Unit 111, extracting the required particulars from the following:**

Ms Joan Brenda Collins of 69 Woodland Avenue, Goring, Leeds LS3 4PS who was born on 22 December 1970 and is British, wishes to enrol for a course in Advanced Wordprocessing. Course Code No is WP 6 and Joan Collins wants to attend evening classes on Mondays and Thursdays. A cheque for £40.50 is enclosed. Today's date please.

- **3** **Fill in the carbon copy of the A4 form you typed in Unit 111, extracting the required particulars from the following:**

Mr John Edward Kramer of 29 Woolgrove Road, LEEDS LS4 6AZ who was born on 12 January 1968 and is American, wishes to enrol for a course in Intermediate German. The Course Code No is G12 and Mr Kramer wishes to attend day classes on Tuesdays and Fridays. A cheque for £50.00 is enclosed. Use tomorrow's date

Shoulder headings

1 **Shoulder headings** always start at the left margin position, and are followed by one clear line of space before the start of the related paragraph.

2 Shoulder headings may be in capital letters (with or without underscoring); with initial capitals (underscored); or in bold type. Follow the style given in the copy.

3 Shoulder headings can be followed by blocked or indented paragraphs – which may be typed in single, 1½, or double spacing.

4 Leave at least one line of space (consistently) between the end of a paragraph and the next shoulder heading.

● 1 **Warm-up drill**
   (*apostrophe*)

The boys' choice was between 4 of the grocer's best Cox's apples at 22p each and 2 of the baker's cakes at 44p each. It didn't take them long to go for the apples. For health and enjoyment, wouldn't you have done the same?

● 2 **A4 paper * side margins 1″ * top margin 2″ * shoulder headings bold with electronic machines.**

BRIGHTER FILING FROM WESTWOOD   *one extra line of space*

Westwood office files are ~~all~~ available in five bright colours (blue, red, green, yellow and orange). This allows colour coding for five different purposes and also helps brighten the ~~modern~~ office environment.

Westwood Lever Arch Files

The space-saving Rado clip ensures that the file stays firmly closed on the shelf.
The ~~hard-wearing~~ *tough* PVC coated covers are easily wiped clean, and the files are fully shoed to prevent scuffing. Available in A4 or foolscap size.

Westwood Box Files

All box files are available with dropside or lockspring. A4 or foolscap size. Standard index A-Z made from top-quality cream manilla - packs of ten, shrink wrapped at special bargain price.

Westwood Expanding Wallets

Strengthened expanding wallets in foolscap size with reinforced gussets and covers. The PVC *coated* covers are easily wiped clean. 20 pockets.

● 3 **Type the above a second time * main heading in spaced capitals, underscored * shoulder headings in capital letters without underscoring * paragraphs in double spacing * top margin 1½″.**

SI 1.28

● 4 **A/S 26** (2 minutes)

That we should read a good newspaper has been impressed upon us all since our youth. But it really is sound advice. Not only do we need to keep abreast of events in our own country and in the world, but what the news means is made clearer in ·leading articles and features.

| 1 | 2 | 3 | 4 | 5 | 6 | 7 | 8 | 9 | 10 | 11 | 12 |

concur confer consul concave concern concept confess contain
disarm dismay disown disable discard discuss disdain disgust

● 2 **Type the following form on A4 paper * one carbon copy. (You will fill them in in Unit 112.)**

REDFORD ADULT CENTRE

Enrolment form
(F)

Surname . . . . (Mr/Mrs/Miss/Ms)*

First name(s) . . . .

Address . . . .

. . . .

. . . . Postcode . . . . . .

Date of birth . . . . Nationality . . . .

Subject of course . . . . Elementary)*
Intermediate) ← (single spacing)
Advanced)

Course code number . . . .

State Day/Evening classes*
and days required . . . .
(as given in the prospectus)

. . . .

. . . .

I enclose a cheque/postal order* for . . . .

Signed . . . .

Date . . . .

*Delete as appropriate

Footnotes

1 **Footnotes** are notes of comment or explanation that are separated from the main text.
2 Where a document contains only one footnote, the asterisk * is generally used as a footnote sign.
3 *a* Most machines have an asterisk key (already raised above the typing line).
  b Otherwise use small letter x with a hyphen typed through it. This made-up asterisk should be *raised half a space in the text,* but not in the footnote itself.
4 In the text there is *no space* between the word concerned and the footnote sign. In the footnote itself there is *one space* after the footnote sign.
5 The footnote is sometimes separated from the main text by an unbroken (underscored) line running from margin to margin, with at least one line of space above and below it. Without this line, the footnote is separated from the text by at least one line of space.
6 If the footnote runs to more than one line, it is typed as a blocked paragraph (always in single spacing) running the full width of the typing line.

- **1 Warm-up drill**
  (*shift keys*)

  aA bB cC dD eE fF gG hH iI jJ kK lL mM nN oO pP qQ rR sS tT
  uU vV wW xX yY zZ aA bB cC dD eE fF gG hH iI jJ kK lL mM nN

- **2 A4 paper * side margins 1″ * top margin 2″**

THE MAYNARD Drawing Officentre← all in caps

of equipment

We offer a ~~compt~~ wide choice / for the professional drawing
office, ~~including the following,~~ at competitive prices*
including the following:

<u>Plan Chest</u> Top-value, sturdy, 6-drawer plan chest
w. hardwood veneer. To take A0 size material – £200,
A1 size material – £159.

<u>Drawing Stand</u> Ideal for both commercial & student use.
Folds flat for easy storage. Complete w. A0 or A1 size
board & counterweight (wire) parallel motion.
Adjustable for angle & height, A0 size – £135, A1 size – £119.

<u>Draughtsman's Chair</u> Posture chair, w. gas-lift, fully
adjustable ~~for~~ from sitting position. Strong, stable aluminium
base w. footrest. £95.

<u>Metal Vertical Filing Cabinet</u> in hammertone grey. Holds up
to 600 drawings. Lockable lid. £400.

<u>Industrial Plan Filing Cabinet</u> Similar to above but w.
skeletal construction & hinged front framework for easy access
to suspended sheets. Takes up very little space. Dust cover. £145.

*All prices include delivery.

(COUNTERWEIGHT)

- **3 Type the above a second time, using shoulder headings * top margin 1½″.**

  SI 1.35

- **4 A/S 27** (2 minutes)

  One of the merits of learning to type is that your skill can
  be put to good personal use. Typed letters are easy to read
  and in business matters tend to get better attention. Often
  it is handy to keep a carbon copy of what was said. One can
  readily think of further uses.

  | 1 | 2 | 3 | 4 | 5 | 6 | 7 | 8 | 9 | 10 | 11 | 12 |

- 1 **Warm-up drill**
  (top row
  letters)

  With typewriter and a quire of paper we were quite equipped.
  Poor Roy is no quitter; he will try to pay what he owes you.

- 2 **Fill in the top copy of the A5 form you typed in Unit 109, using the following particulars,
  and today's date. Type the message you took as a blocked paragraph.**

Call at 1015 hrs for B Dasgupta from Mary Evans of
Fosters Transport, Ship Street, Brighton
(Tel 0273 25831). Long delays in Channel crossings will
result from yesterday's lightning 24-hour seamen's
  at Newhaven   urgent
strike/. Therefore our/container consignment of
rehicle spare parts (Job No 642 Q) cannot be shipped
to Dieppe until tomorrow at the earliest. It is, however,
being given top priority.

- 3 **Fill in the carbon copy of the A5 form you typed in Unit 109, using the following particulars,
  and today's date. Type the message you took as a blocked paragraph.**

Call at 1530 hrs for Mr Masters from Dr Kurt Adler, our agent
in Hamburg (Tel 010 49 40 63212). The week suggested for
your visit to Hamburg is entirely suitable. When the
                          + send you
dates are firm, Dr Adler will prepare/a programme of
bus. and social engagements. Yr. early confirmation
wd be appreciated.

Word division

1 **Word division** at the end of lines is not essential in general work. However there *are* times when it is necessary.
 a When justifying text to achieve an exactly even right-hand margin, the text needs to be keyed in as far along the typing line as possible, ie finishing as close up to the right margin setting as you can. Then there is less 'spare space' to be distributed evenly along the line when the machine automatically justifies – and an unduly drawn-out appearance is avoided.
 b When typing on a card, etc, shortage of space may make it necessary to fill up the typing line.

2 You should therefore learn how to divide words at a suitable point. The guidelines are based on common sense and the effect the word-break will have on easy reading. The dividing hyphen must always be at the *end of the line*, never at the beginning of the next line with the part-word carried over.

3 Follow these **guidelines** and divide:
 a according to spoken sound (win-dow, pic-ture).
 b at an existing permanent hyphen – and there only (self-reliant, pre-arrange).
 c between two words forming a single word (mantel-piece, ginger-bread).
 d between double consonants (admit-tance, neces-sary).
 e according to pronunciation when 3 consonants come together (scram-bling, trium-phant).
 f after a prefix (trans-fer, sub-marine) or before a suffix (pain-less, knowledge-able).
 g in long words as near as possible to the right margin setting (admin-admini-, administra- for administration).
 (Many words can be divided in more than one place.)

4 Do *not* divide:
 a words of one syllable (through, thoughts).
 b so that only two letters are carried to the next line (quick-ly, wait-ed).
 c abbreviations (UNESCO, O & M).
 d figures (£5,456.85, 12,643,850).
 e dates (12 January 1990) or personal names (Mr G Henderson).
 f on more than two consecutive lines.

● 1 **Warm-up drill**
 (*one-hand*
 words)

```
far, pin, war, him, bed, joy, cat, nip, vat, hip, axe, hop,
fear, monk, were, hulk, bear, plum, card, kiln, pony, dart,
add, kill, dagger, noon, barred, pool, dabbed, pull, added.
```

● 2 **A4 paper * set a tab stop 25 spaces to the right of the left margin setting * copy the words one to a line down the paper in 1½ line spacing * as you finish each word, use the tabulator to take you to the tab stop position to type the word again. This time insert a hyphen where you can divide the word, eg practice prac-tice. If the word should not be divided, repeat it in its original form.**

```
practice   broadsheet   half-term   paragraph   boardroom   suspense
lasting   self-supporting   excellent   brought   garden   £60,482.64
Mrs A Winterbottom   landscape   first-class   constant   groundless
UNRRA   translate   disgust   electrical   backbone   fumbling
permission   programme   market   allotted   statistics   NALGO
fraction   well-behaved   underlined   pressure   stumbled   chairperson
```

● 3 **Type again task 2 in Unit 38 * keep right margin *as even as possible* with word division * justify if your machine can automatically perform this function.**

SI 1.34

● 4 **A/S 28** (2 minutes)

```
Most firms choose with great care the person whose job it is
to answer the telephone.  They realise that he or she should
have a pleasant speaking voice and always be most polite and
helpful in manner.  No one should be left waiting at the end
of a line without explanation.
```

| 1| 2| 3| 4| 5| 6| 7| 8| 9| 10| 11| 12|

Forms

Skeleton forms Sometimes you may need to start some details part-way across the page (set a tab stop). Ensure that the insertion lines are long enough to take the information that is likely to be typed or written on them.

- 1 **Warm-up drill**
  (bottom row words)

  can cox cave cavern comb combine cannibal convince vex vixen
  venom vacuum vaccine voice box bomb buzz brave become became

- 2 **Type the Telephone Message form on A5 portrait paper * take one carbon copy. (You will fill them in in Unit 110.)**

U N I V E R S A L   T R A D I N G   G R O U P

EXPORT DEPARTMENT

Telephone Message

Call for .... Date ....

Caller .... Time ....

.... Tel No ....

....

....

Message

Call taken by ....

Correcting ringed errors

1 Sometimes you will be asked to **retype documents that contain errors**. At Level 1 you will not be expected to find the errors yourself. Each word, etc, containing an error will be ringed: you have to decide what is wrong and correct it.
2 The kinds of error to look for are: typing errors (including spacing faults), obvious errors in agreement ('was' for 'were' etc) punctuation errors (including apostrophe).
3 When retyping, take care you do not make any new errors!

● 1 **Warm-up drill**
   (*shift keys, comma*)

Amy, Bob, Con, Dan, Eve, Fred, Gert, Hugh, Ida, Jet, Ken, Liz, Mo, Ned, Olga, Pam, Quin, Rose, Sid, Ted, Una, Vera, Win, Xavier, Yves, Zena.

● 2 **Retype on A4 paper correcting the ringed errors * double spacing * decide your own side and top margins to present a balanced appearance on the page.**

BUYING YOUR OWN HOME

A Solid Investment

High inflation over recent decades has considerably decreased the value of saving's that pay a fixed rate of interest - bank deposit accounts, building society accounts, etc. People who invested thier money in buying their own home have much more to show for their money.

Property values has doubled over the last few years, and it can now be difficult for first-time buyers to enter the market. But it is worth buying your first home if you can, as soon as you have a steady job.

It may require taking out a high mortgage-but you get tax relief on this, and you will be repaying the mortgage with money thatis decreasing in value all the time. There appears to be no end to the upward spiral in house prices - so get in as soon as you can. Apart from the financial considerations, the satisfaction of owning and renovating your own home can be considerably.

SI 1.37

● 3 **A/S 29** (2 minutes)

There are many good reasons why holidays abroad are popular. One of them is simply that it is refreshing to live for even a short time in a strange country and learn its customs. As knowledge of the language is so useful, it is worth learning some common words and phrases.

| 1| 2| 3| 4| 5| 6| 7| 8| 9| 10| 11| 12|

UNIVERSAL HOTELS CHAIN

Type on plain A4 paper

Another year of growth

* Earnings per share increased by 12% — & doubled in the last 5 years.
* Fixed assets now exceed £1,500 million.
* Dividends per share increased by 10%.
* The policy of investing significant sums in the maintenance & upgrading of the Co's existing properties has continued.
* 3,000 new jobs were created during the yr.
* The Co is in the forefront of promoting tourism & stimulating foreign earnings f the country.
* The new/financial year has started well & we look forward to the rest of the year with confidence.

RESULTS
(Year to 31 October 19--)

last year   *year before last*

	19-- £m	19-- £m
Sales	1,4765	1,244.5
Gross Trading Profit	207.0	184.3
Profit before tax	136.0	129.6
Profit attributable to shareholders	97.1	86.7
Earnings per share (net)	12.42p	11.11p
Dividends per share	6.00p	5.45p

For reservations at any of our hotels worldwide, ring our booking office on 01-474 89602, contact your local travel agent, or ring the hotel direct.

MANTON COLLEGE GAMES CHAMPIONSHIP

Position	Name	Points
1	G Brown	68
2	D West	67
3	P Rogers	59
4	C Wilcox	54
5	R Singh	45
6	S Archer	42
7	L Philips	37
8	B Charles	33
9-10	F Goldstein	19
9	E Davis	28

Type on A5 paper

Insetting

1 **Insetting (indenting) from the left margin** is a technique used to draw the reader's attention to the inset text – which stands out clearly from the rest.
2 When the inset text uses **different line spacing** from the main text, the highlighting effect is even more marked.
3 Insetting can be used to draw attention to key lines, to quote extracts from other documents, and for numbered/lettered listed items (Unit 42).
4 If there is no specific instruction, inset the given text 5 character spaces from the left margin-set.
5 On electronic machines use the indent function. Otherwise either:
   a Change the left margin-set to the inset position (Do not forget to move back afterwards.) Use this method if the inset text is lengthy.
   b Use the tabulator on every line of the inset text.

● 1 **Warm-up drill**
   (*whole alphabet*)

A baker's dozen is an expression for 13. Squaring the circle is a way of describing the impossible. Rough justice is very. hasty judgment.

● 2 **A4 paper * double spacing * decide own margins (wide) so matter will be centrally positioned on paper * keep an even right-hand margin * justify if your machine has this facility * centre the two top and bottom lines.**

ACCLAIM SYSTEMS← (spaced caps)

FOR CARPET AND UPHOLSTERY CLEANING YOU CAN TRUST

To introduce our services to householders in yr area, we are offering 30% off our normal prices for one month only. We are the professionals you can trust to clean yr furnishings + carpets – correctly – safely← (use dashes) – thoroughly. Our cleaning processes involve:

(Inset 5 spaces – in single spacing please)
Deep extraction cleaning, removing ground-in dirt + grit. Colours and brightness restored. Stale odours removed + replaced w. a fresh-as-spring smell. No sticky detergent residues.

We wl. leave yr furnishings looking nearly as good as new. All work is guaranteed. We now clean a 3-piece suite for ONLY £42.50 and carpets (average lounge/diner, hall, stairs) for ONLY £44.50. Other estimates provided free.
DON'T DELAY — RING US TODAY!
Telephone : 01-695 3127

SI 1.39

● 3 **A/S 30** (2 minutes)

Many people do not use the public libraries or know the full range of services which they provide. Lending libraries not only offer the books on their shelves, but if asked will get others for home reading. Most reference sections have books on a broad range of questions.

| 1 | 2 | 3 | 4 | 5 | 6 | 7 | 8 | 9 | 10 | 11 | 12 |

WP Assignment 5. *Key-in* document (FORM) for 10-pitch print-out. Remember to use the RETURN key at the end of repeater key insertion lines. *Text-edit* Line 4: change 'Name' to 'Name in full' (followed by one space). Line 7: change 'Age' to 'Date of birth' (followed by one space). *Proof-read* text on screen and correct. *Print-out* one copy in 10-pitch.

TWEEDWORTH WOOLLENS LIMITED, WILMINGTON

Application for Employment

Type on A4 paper in treble spacing

Position applied for ....

Name ....

Address ....

....

Age ....

Examinations passed ....

....

Previous employment with details ....

....

....

....

....

....

Outside interests ....

Referees (1) ....

       (2) ....

....

Task 6

Transfer the following particulars to your typed form

Alison Johnson of 21 Herne Road, Wilmington, Kent is applying for a position as a typist at Tweedworth Woollens Limited. She is 17 years old and has passed GCSE's in English, Mathematics and History: she has also passed the RSA stage II Typewriting examination. This would be Alison's first job and she is interested in Photography, Reading and Travel. The following have agreed to act as referees on her behalf:

    The Rev George Wade, The Rectory, Wilmington
    Mr D L Black, Headmaster, Wilmington Secondary School

Listed items

1 **Numbered/lettered listed items** are included in many documents for ease of reference and clarity of meaning.

2 A **consistent method** should be used within a document – the numbers or letters typed with or without a following full stop, enclosed in brackets, or with just a right-hand bracket. Roman numerals should be blocked to the right or left. Always follow the style of listing shown in the draft.

1.	1	(1)	1)	(a)	i	i	Lift the receiver.	(4 spaces)
2.	2	(2)	2)	(b)	ii or	ii	Listen for the dial tone.	(3 spaces)
3.	3	(3)	3)	(c)	iii	iii	Dial the required number.	(2 spaces)

3 **Spacing** between the numbers/letters and the start of the text must be consistent within a document (2 or 3 spaces). Special care is needed with roman numerals, particularly when blocked left (as shown above).

4 **Insetting** Sometimes numbered/lettered items are inset from the left margin.

• 1 **Warm-up drill**
(*hyphen*)

This 18-page leaflet contains an up-to-date list of all our full-time, part-time, and day-release courses in Computing and Word-processing.

• 2 **A4 paper * double spacing * decide own margins.**

PAY NEGOTIATIONS
19-- to 19--

In this yr's pay negotiations the Co. just cannot afford to go beyond the wage and salary increases already offered. We are however ready to discuss marginal improvements in conditions of service under the following headings:

Indent 5 spaces + use single spacing →

(a) Higher rate of productivity bonus
(b) Attendance bonus
(c) Longer holidays
(d) Improved sickness benefits (industrial injury)
(e) Improved maternity leave + benefits

It is hoped that a settlement on these lines can soon be reached to put an end to the present disruptions. // We need to considerably improve our competitiveness + share of the market before any future pay increases can even be considered.

24 October 19--
SJK

• 3 **Type task 2 again * use small roman numerals without brackets instead of letters for the listed items * adjust margins if you wish to improve your placement on the paper * do not inset the numbered items.**

(Type on A5 paper)

WP Assignment 4. *Key-in* document (AUCTION) for 10-pitch print-out. Use block centring function to centre all lines in one operation instead of each line separately. Dates and times in bold. *Text-edit* Line 13: insert 'choice' between 'A' and 'collection', and start 'clocks' and 'barometers' with initial capitals. Line 15: insert 'Valuable' before 'oriental'. (Lines 13 and 15 will need re-centring). *Proof-read* text on screen and correct. *Print-out* 2 copies in 10-pitch.

GRAHAM EDWARDS & COMPANY
incorporating
LEOPOLD COHEN & SONS
are instructed to offer
For Sale By Auction

(Centre lines using centre function OR block the whole)

at

Hadbrook House, Walsingham

on

27 October at 10.30am

(THE VALUABLE CONTENTS)

including
Fine antique items of English & French Furniture
A collection of clocks and barometers
Silver and Glass
oriental ~~Choice~~ Carpets and Rugs

On view 26 October from 9.30 to 4.30

(Type on A4 paper — double spacing)

EXTRACT FROM MINUTES
OF RECREATION COMMITTEE MEETING
held on 2 May 19--
(Riverdale Recreation Centre)

(based on market research,)

The Cttee resumed consideration of the proposal for the provision of a Recreation Centre on the Riverside site.

PUBLIC INTEREST — Revised figures were produced for the number of residents likely to use the facilities. These left no doubt about the strong interest in the project amongst all sections of the community.

FINANCIAL ASPECTS — On the other hand, the latest estimates showed that the scale of charges required to meet running costs wd prob be excessive.

CONCLUSION — The Cttee decided that the project shd be held over for the present.

Numbering blocked paragraphs

1 Number blocked paragraphs using the following method (but use the indent function if your machine has it).

  a Type each number at the left margin, consistently with or without a following full stop or with bracket(s). Use the style of the copy.
  b Leave (consistently within a document) 2 or 3 character spaces between the number and the start of the blocked paragraphs.
  c Set a tab stop where each line of the blocked paragraphs will start.

The paragraph numbers will then stand out clearly on their own – as shown below.

2 For **lengthy numbered paragraphs**, set the left margin where each line of the blocked paragraphs starts, and backspace into the left margin to type the numbers.

● 1 **Warm-up drill**
   (*whole alphabet*)

● 2 A4 paper

This company treats its qualified staff justly and even generously, but expects zealous work in return.

The Metric System ← *all caps*

A logical feature of the system, based on its decimal structure, is the use of /*standard* prefixes to the names of the /*main* units, eg <u>deci</u>- means one-tenth, <u>centi</u>- means one-hundredth, <u>milli</u>- means one-thousandth, and <u>kilo</u> means one thousand.

1. The metre (just over 3 ft 3 in) is the basic unit of <u>length</u>. Thus a kilometre is a thousand metres, a centimetre is one-hundredth of a metre - and so on.

2. The /*basic* unit of <u>liquid measurement</u> is the litre (just under 2 pints). A decilitre is one-tenth of a litre, a centilitre one-hundredth of a litre, and a millilitre one-thousandth of a litre.

3. The /*basic* unit of <u>weight</u> is the kilogram (less than *slightly* 2 lb 4 oz). A gram is one-thousandth of a kilogram, and a tonne is one thousand kilograms.

SI 1.28

● 3 A/S 31
   (2 minutes)

The good typist should at all times bear in mind the need to save paper. As with most things, however, there is true and false economy. Good work is never crowded on a page. So be careful in choosing the size of paper and avoid false starts and all rash errors which cause whole pages to be destroyed.

WP Assignment 3. *Key-in* letter
(document name BUNGS) for 12-
pitch print-out. Subject heading
and shoulder headings in bold
without underscore. *Text-edit* First
Line: insert 'urgently' between
'were' and 'interested'. Final
sentence: insert 'to be taken' after
'you'. *Proof-read* text on screen
and correct. *Print-out* 2 copies in
12-pitch.

Ref EW. PT. H6903

Mrs B James

20 Mountjoy Ave

LEEDS LS2 4AX

Take 2 ccs and type an envelope

Dear Mrs J—

BUNGALOWS IN THE WOODLANDS AREA

When you telephoned me yesterday you said you were
interested in buying a property in the Woodlands area of
this town, preferably a bungalow with a good-sized garden. The
following are attractive properties in the price range you
indicated.

Pentlands, Longridge Drive, Woodlands

This is a virtually new bung, enjoying open country views
over the Downs. It is soundly built and well appointed. The
accom consist of lounge, dining room, 3 bedrooms,
bathroom & kitchen. There is a well-kept garden of 3/4 acre.
Price: £75,000 freehold

Fernbank, 42 Queen's Road, Woodlands

One of the older bungalows in the district, in the most favoured
area within easy reach of schools and shops. Accom:
lounge/dining-room, 3 bedrooms, study, bathroom &
kitchen. Well stocked garden of 1/2 acre.
Price: £70,000 f/hold

I shall be pleased to arrange for you to view these
properties at yr convenience.
Yrs sinc—
E Willow   Office Manager

From   Office Manager   Ref AST. 8P
To   All clerical/secretarial staff

ECONOMIES IN STATIONARY MATERIALS
Our bill for stationery has risen very sharply during the past
6 months. Some of this increase is, of course, due to inflation but
my attention has been drawn to unnecessary waste — particularly
headed Company paper & envelopes. [I wd urge everyone,
especially the typists, to be as economical as poss in all
stationary matters.

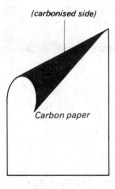

(carbonised side)

Carbon paper

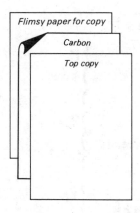

Flimsy paper for copy

Carbon

Top copy

1 **File copy** An exact copy of every letter, etc, sent out is kept for filing/ reference purposes. Carbon copying and photocopying are the most common methods used.

2 **Carbon copying** is still widely used to obtain one or two copies – being simple, immediate and cheap. Its importance is reflected in the fact that public exams require a carbon copy of one document. Therefore you need regular practice in this skill. The carbon copy must be an *accurate copy of the original*, ie all corrections made on the top copy must also be made on the carbon copy.

3 **Carbon paper or plastic film sheets** (obtainable in various colours and sizes) should be handled gently to avoid smudging fingers and papers. Special flimsy (thin) paper is generally used for the carbon copies.

4 **Store carbon paper flat**, preferably in a box away from heat. If creased or wrinkled, carbon paper will produce poor copies. After several uses, cut a thin strip off the top or bottom of the carbon sheet – to ensure that all the carbonised surface is used.

5 **Assembling the papers** Insert the papers into the typewriter so that the carbonised side of the sheet faces the roller. Then use the paper release lever if adjustment of the papers is necessary to evenly align them.

6 **Make corrections** using one of the following methods.

a *Correction fluid* Paint out the error on the top copy, then on the carbon copy. Wait till it is *completely dry* before typing in the correction: otherwise the carbon copy will be unreadable, and fluid transferred to the carbon paper will produce a 'blank' patch when next you use it.

b *Correction paper/film strips* A special type is available for use with carbon copies. When the error has been typed again through the strip, it is removed (from both top and carbon copy) and the correction typed in.

c *Lift-off tape* Slip a piece of protecting paper between the carbon paper and the carbon copy (to prevent overtyping on the carbon copy) while you correct the top copy with the lift-off tape. Remove from the machine, remove error(s) from the carbon copy with fluid or rubber, reinsert the carbon copy into machine and type in correction(s).

d *Rubber* Before erasing on the top copy, insert a slip of protecting paper between the carbon paper and the flimsy at the point of the error. Then remove the paper and erase the error on the carbon copy. Type in correction.

7 **Photocopying** is the method used in many offices whatever the number of copies needed. It is considered more efficient than taking and correcting carbon copies. Photocopying has the advantage that it produces a high-quality *identical* copy of the original in seconds.

● 1 **Warm-up drill**
(*whole alphabet*)

The driver was lucky that he was only quite lightly injured when the express train jumped the frozen rails at the sharp bend in the track.

● 2 **Type again task 2 in Unit 43 with one carbon copy.**

SI 1.32

● 3 **A/S 32**
(2 minutes)

It is truly said that any good·typist must be able to spell. It should be added that anyone keen to be a typist can learn to spell. Often people who spell badly are not aware of the fact. So we must test our spelling by watching the words as we read books and daily newspapers. Practice makes perfect.

| 1| 2| 3| 4| 5| 6| 7| 8| 9| 10| 11| 12|

1. A special **Chairperson's Agenda** with notes for his/her benefit under relevant items is often prepared by the Secretary, to assist the efficient running of the meeting.
2. The right-hand half of the page is left blank for the Chairperson to add additional notes of his/her own.
3. Divide the two halves of the page (approximately) by a brace (right-hand bracket) setting a tab stop at the brace position.
4. Always leave at least one space between the type and the brace.
5. Repeat the Agenda numbers (for additional notes) to the right-hand side of the brace (two spaces between the brace and the numbers).

- **1 Warm-up drill**
  (alternate hand words)

nook read oil safe poll tea upon vase you wader hill are ink
beds jump cart kip dew loop erred milk fades noun grass oily

- **2 A4 paper * one carbon copy**

WP Assignment 2. *Key-in* document (CHAGENDA) for 12-pitch print-out. Numbered shoulder headings in bold with underscore (use automatic numbering function if available). *Text-edit* Change 'Valley Hotel' to 'Town Hall'. At end of items 4 and 5 insert '(attached)'. *Proof-read* text on screen, and correct. *Print-out* 2 copies in 12-pitch.

CRAIGHALL RESIDENTS ASSOCIATION
Meeting to be held in the Valley Hotel on Tuesday
24 September 19-- at 7.30 pm

CHAIRMAN'S AGENDA ← (spaced caps)
1. Apologies for absence   ) 1.
   Vice-chairman still in hospital but   )
   doing well.   )
2. Minutes of last meeting   ) 2.
   Secretary regrets omission of Mr Brown's)
   name under those present.   )
3. Matters arising from the minutes   ) 3.
   Any attempt to re-open the cycle path   )
   issue shd be disallowed.   )
4. Pedestrian crossing in Oak Road   ) 4.
   Council is resisting on grounds of   )
   proximity to Beech Rd crossing. See   )
   letter of 3 September.   )
5. Conversion of the Crown Hotel   ) 5.
   Miss King's scheme for an old   )
   people's home ~~see~~ seems   )
   impracticable — see Council's letter   )
   of 12 September.   )
6. Any other business   ) 6.
7. Date of next meeting   ) 7.
   Chairman and Secretary both away   )
   on the last Tuesday in Oct. Suggest   )
   following Tuesday.   )

1 **'A' paper sizes** are shown below with their metric measurements. The sizes most used in offices are A4, A5 and A6. A5 is exactly half A4 size, and A6 is exactly half A5 size. Used *portrait* means with the shorter side at the top, used *landscape* with the longer side at the top.

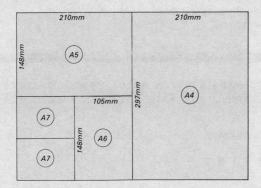

Horizontal scales
Pica type (10-pitch) 10 spaces = 25 mm (1″)
Elite type (12-pitch) 12 spaces = 25 mm (1″)

Vertical scale
6 lines in single spacing (pica and elite) = 25 mm (1″)

2 **A4 paper (approx 8¼″ × 11¾″)**

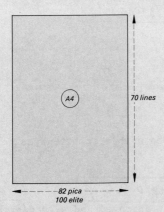

A4 margins should be not less than 25 mm (1″) at the top, bottom, and left: and not less than 12 mm (½″) at the right. Thus:
1″ left and ½″ right margins: pica at 10 and 77
                           : elite at 12 and 94
1″ left and 1″ right margins : pica at 10 and 72
                           : elite at 12 and 88

3 **A5 portrait paper (approx 5⅞″ × 8¼″)**

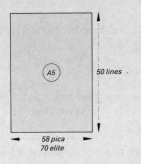

A5 portrait margins should be not less than 12 mm (½″) all round (top, bottom, right and left). Thus:
½″ left and ½″ right margins: pica at 5 and 53
                           : elite at 6 and 64
¾″ left and ½″ right margins: pica at 7 and 53
                           : elite at 9 and 64
¾″ left and ¾″ right margins: pica at 7 and 51
                           : elite at 9 and 61

● 1 **Warm-up drill**
(*top row characters*)

In their advertisement, Brent & Rogers (Carriers) Ltd of 24/28 High Street claimed 'lowest rates in the City'. Yet they charged £50.50 to remove my few bits of furniture only 2 miles! What do you think of that?

● 2 **Take two sheets of A4 paper and cut one of them in half to make two A5 sheets * using the A4 and an A5 sheet, check the sizes and scales given above * then stick one A5 sheet in the middle of the A4 sheet (both portrait) and rule round the edges of the A5 with ruler and ball-point pen * within the bounds of the A4 and the A5, write their respective scales, etc, given above * keep this sheet to hand for easy reference later on.**

Minutes

1 The **Minutes of a Meeting** should be a brief, accurate and clear record of the proceedings and decisions of the meeting.
2 Topics are dealt with in the order of the meeting (as in the Agenda), and numbered.
3 The names of those attending the meeting head the Minutes, the Chairperson's name appearing first.

- 1 **Warm-up drill**
  (one hand only lines)

Eager stags traversed westward deserts after water reserves. Molly, hop on my pony. Minny, you join Polly in Kimono Inn.

- 2 **Use A4 paper * use numbered shoulder headings as shown.**

M I N U T E S   O F   M E E T I N G

A meeting of the Entertainments Committee of the Shoreland Traders Association was held on Wednesday 12 January 19-- at 1800 hrs. *in the Committee Room of the Council Offices*

PRESENT

Mr S Lentern (Chair~~man~~ *person*)
Mr T Benham
Miss A West
Mr P Neames (Secretary)

1. APOLOGIES FOR ABSENCE

The (Secretary) reported that Mr Mountain was unable to attend as he was out of the country on business .

2. MINUTES OF LAST MEETING

The Minutes of the last meeting *, held on 10 Oct. 19--,* were read, approved and signed bythe Chair~~man~~ *person*.

3. MATTERS ARISING FROM ~~THE~~ MINUTES

The Secretary reported that the application for a bar licence at this year's Annual Dinner and Dance had been aproved.

4. ARRANGEMENTS FOR ~~THE~~ ANNUAL DINNER AND DANCE

Miss West announced that she had made arrangements for the Paul Smithson Group to play at a fee of £200. She also stated that the printing of tickets was in progress.

After a lengthy discussion it was agreed to increase the price of a double ticket to £21.00.

5. A O B ← *in full*
There was no other business.

6. NEXT MTG
The date + time of the next meeting was fixed for 15 April 19-- at 1800 hrs.
The Chair~~man~~ person declared the mtg closed at 1950 hrs.

Chair~~man~~ person ------------------- *Date* ----------

- 3 **Type above Minutes a second time on A4 paper * use numbered marginal headings.**

Longer accuracy/speed timings You should now proceed to using regularly the 4–10 minute A/S timings in Unit 137 (pages 167–177). Start in this Unit.

Leaving space of specified size A competent typist must be able to use the machine to measure a space of specified size to be left anywhere on the page, eg for the later insertion of a bar chart, pie chart, illustration, etc. It might be a space of stated depth extending across the whole page, or a square or rectangle occupying only part of the page width. This is a straightforward matter once the basic scales given in Unit 45 are known.

1 *Calculating vertical space* (lines down the page) Leave 6 lines of space for each 25 mm (1"). Thus to leave a space 25 mm (1") deep, turn up 7 times in single spacing. (You will *type* on the 7th line.) To leave 50 mm (2") turn up 13 times, and so on.

2 *Calculating horizontal space* (character spaces *across* the page) For each 25 mm (1") leave: 10 character spaces with pica (10-pitch) type
12 character spaces with elite (12-pitch) type

Use the paper bail scale or other paper scale when making calculations.

3 If the space you are asked to leave is not *exactly* specified, it is advisable to leave 1 or 2 extra lines *down* and 2 or 3 extra character spaces *across*.

● 1 **Warm-up drill**
(*figures*)

a1 s2 d3 f4 f5 j6 j7 k8 19 ;0 a1 s2 d3 f4 f5 j6 j7 k8 19 ;0

● 2 **Use A4 paper * double spacing * top margin 1½" * side margins 1".**

LONGFELLOW GROUP plc

Half-year ended 30 Sept 19--

The Group continued to achieve a healthy rate of growth in the first 6 mths of the current financial year. Sales increased by 14.3 per cent to £1,087.0 m, + at £142.8 m the pre-tax profit was 12.1 per cent higher than in the corresponding period last yr.

Typist - leave here an unruled space for insertion of a graph measuring 2½ inches (62 mm) × 2½ inches

Interim dividend (last yr's figures in brackets) The directors have ~~declared~~ decided an interim div per ordinary share of 5.1 p (4.6 p) totalling £36.8 m (£33.1 m).
Currency exchange rates In accordance w the Group's normal practice at the interim stage, the results of overseas cos. for the half-yr have been translated into sterling at the rates of exchange ruling at 31 March, except for the results of cos. in Brazil + Mexico which have bn translated into sterling at 30 Sept rates of exchange. If the rates of exchange at 30 Sept had bn applied to the interim results of all overseas cos, turnover wd have increased by £56.6 m and profit before taxation by £7.7 m.

27 Nov 19--

Shareholders meetings of a limited company or plc Such meetings documents are very formal in tone. Where applicable, information to shareholders about such matters as voting rights (including proxy voting), dividends, etc, is given.

- **1 Warm-up drill**
  (figures)

  a1 s2 d3 f4 f5 j6 j7 k8 19 ;0 a1 s2 d3 f4 f5 j6 j7 k8 19 ;0

- **2 Type the following on A4 paper.**

THE CENTRAL ENGINEERING COMPANY LIMITED

ANNUAL GENERAL MEETING ← *initial caps + underscored*

NOTICE IS HEREBY GIVEN that the Ninth Annual General Meeting of the Company will be held in the Rochester Hall, Hill Place, Coventry, on Tuesday 24 May 19-- at 1100 hrs.

B U S I N E S S

1 To receive and consider the Directors' Report, Accounts and Balance Sheet for the year ended 31 March 19--.

3 To declare an Ordinary Final Dividend.

2 To confirm the Preference Dividend paid in August 19-- and the Ordinary Interim Dividend paid in September 19--.

4 To confirm the transfer of £2,250,000 to General Reserve.

5 To elect 2 Directors.

6 To transact any other business that may be brought before an Ordinary General Meeting.

BY ORDER OF THE BOARD

G Basra
Secretary

21 March 19--

Open punctuation

1 **Open punctuation** reduces punctuation marks to a minimum. As a general rule, only punctuation that is essential to convey meaning and clarity to the reader is retained. This means that punctuation marks are omitted:

   a after abbreviations.
   b at the end of lines at the head and foot of letters.
   c at the end of lines on envelopes, postcards, etc.

2 **Time** Note that even in open punctuation style, a full stop is used to separate hours and minutes when using the 12-hour clock (11.45 am, 2.20 pm) but not usually with the 24-hour method (1145 hrs, 1420 hrs).

3 Some examples of open punctuation follow, and you should study them carefully. They are also given with full punctuation *for comparison only*.

Open punctuation	**Full punctuation**
NB Raincoats, etc, are needed.	N.B. Raincoats, etc., are needed.
Mr T S Waters BSc works here.	Mr. T. S. Waters, B.Sc., works here.
Come at 7.20 pm, not 8.20 pm.	Come at 7.20 p.m., not 8.20 p.m.
12 January 1990	12th January, 1990.
RSVP (meaning 'please reply')	R.S.V.P.
PLC or plc (meaning 'public limited company')	P.L.C. or p.l.c.
Mrs G Smith BA	Mrs. G. Smith, B.A.,
24 Lime Avenue	24 Lime Avenue,
BRADFORD	BRADFORD.
BD6 8GK	BD6 8GK

(Note that the postcode is never punctuated in any way)

- **1 Copy, line by line, the open punctuation examples given above, paying special attention to punctuation and spacing.**

- **2 A5 portrait paper * single spacing * side margins ¾″ and ½″ * top margin 1½″.**

DENTON COLLEGE ← Spaced caps
Essay Competition ← Caps
Christmas 19 - -

Entries for the competition must be delivered before 6.45 pm on 20 Dec. 19 - - to :

Mr R S Chambers MA
Flat 3
Langley Hall
BRISTOL   BS8 3JB

Inset 5 spaces

The rules of the competition + the choice of subjects have been displayed on all noticeboards since 1 November. // The judges wl take into a/c the age of entrants + the courses, etc, they have attended both long + short term. This information shd therefore be given with the on the entry form that accompanies the essay

3 December 19 - -
RSC/JTK

- **1 Warm-up drill**
  (alphabet/comma)

  a, b, c, d, e, f, g, h, i, j, k, l, m, n, o, p, q, r, s, t,
  u, v, w, x, y, z, a, b, c, d, e, f, g, h, i, j, k, l, m, n,

- **2 Type the following Notice of Meeting on A5 paper.**

CRAIGHALL RESIDENTS ASSOCIATION

The next meeting of the Association will be held
in the Valley Hotel, Craighall, on ~~Wednesday~~
~~25 September~~ 19-- at 7.30 pm. The Agenda will
be circulated later.

Correct to Tuesday 24 September please

Roger Steel
Hon Secretary

24 Greenhill Gardens
Craighall (Tel 3976)

10 Sept 19--

- **3 Type the related Agenda on A5 paper.**

CRAIGHALL R— A—

Meeting to be held in the Valley Hotel,
Craighall, on Tues 24 Sept 19 —
at 7.30 pm.

AGENDA← *(spaced caps)*

1. Apologies for absence
2. Minutes of last meeting
3. Matters arising fr the Mins
4. Pedestrian crossing in Oak Rd
5. Conversion of the Crown Hotel
6. A O B← *in full please — Any Other Business*
7. Next meeting

R— S—
H— Sec—

15 Sept 19 —

Typing envelopes

1 **Envelopes** should be typed with each part of the address on a separate line, with the town in capital letters.

2 The postcode is the last item to be typed on an envelope and is usually on a separate line. It is typed with one space between its two parts; it should not be punctuated or underlined. Where the postcode is not on a separate line, leave 2 spaces in front of it.

3 FOR THE ATTENTION OF, CONFIDENTIAL, URGENT, etc, are typed above the name and address, separated by one line of space. Use closed capitals, underscoring or bold type.

4 REGISTERED POST, RECORDED DELIVERY, etc, are typed in capitals in the top *left* corner.

5 The name and address should be typed along the longer side of the envelope.

6 Start typing approximately half way down the envelope and approximately one-third in from the left edge. (Use a pencil × guide till you are practised and can manage without it.)

7 For speed use the blocked method and single spacing. 1½″ or double spacing can be used on extra large envelopes.

```
      PERSONAL

      Mrs S Cole
      42 Court Road
      MANCHESTER
      M16 6AL
```

```
RECORDED DELIVERY


      Mr T L Bond
      25 Longton Road
      EXETER
      Devon
      EX5 2PQ
```

```
      Watford Fine Decorators
      8 Lee Rise
      WATFORD
      Herts
      WD3 4AP
```

```
      Urgent

      Miss C Day
      26 West Road
      LONDON SW9 5ET
```

● 1 **Warm-up drill**
  (*whole alphabet*)

The signs of the zodiac are named after constellations. Examples are Libra and Aquarius. In what is called judicial astrology, their movements are supposed to influence luck and fortune.

● 2 **Copy the above numbered paragraphs on A5 portrait paper * use the heading TYPING ENVELOPES * side margins ¾″ and ½″ * top margin 1½″.**

● 3 **Use C6 envelopes (114 mm × 162 mm, 4½″ × 6⅜″) to type the four addresses shown above * alternatively use A4 paper folded into 4 * use all the 'faces' * do *not* use single slips of C6 size paper: they are difficult to use and do not give the correct 'feel'.**

Notice and agenda

Regular meetings held by organisations and committees often follow a set pattern of documents. These are: Notice of Meeting, Agenda, and Minutes of Meeting. The Notice of Meeting and Agenda are sometimes combined in one document.

1 **Notice of Meeting** A copy is sent by the Secretary to everyone entitled to attend. It states the day, time, place, and sometimes the purpose of the meeting.

2 **The Agenda** is prepared by the Secretary in consultation with the Chairperson. It lists the items to be dealt with at the meeting, in the order they will be taken. The Agenda is usually sent out beforehand so that everyone has advance notice of what is to be discussed.

3 **Layout style** may be fully blocked as shown in the following pages *or* headings, etc, may be centred.

● 1 **Warm-up drill**
   (whole alphabet)

It must be just exasperating for foreigners to learn a language like ours in which tough, bough, cough, dough and through are all pronounced quite differently. Or take laughter and daughter; foul and soul; monkey and donkey; zeal and zealous; over and cover!

● 2 **Type the following combined Notice and Agenda of Meeting on A5 paper.**

BIDMOUTH SPORTS CLUB

The Annual General Meeting of the Bidmouth Sports Club will be held at the White Swan Inn, Bidmouth, on Tuesday 20 March 19-- at ~~1930~~ hrs.
                                       1900

A G E N D A

1. Apologies for absence

2. Minutes of last meeting

3. Matters arising therefrom
                Chairperson's
4. ~~Chairman's~~ Annual Report

5. Treasurer's Annual Report and Balance Sheet

6.7. Any other business

7.6. Plans for extending the Club's facilities

8. Date, time, and place of next meeting

        Thomas
   ~~T~~/Helpman
   Hon Secretary

9 March 19--

1 **Courtesy titles** (eg Mr, Mrs, Miss) are used on envelopes and on letters which are addressed to a person by his/her surname. Most are typed as abbreviations.	Miss L Barker Mrs B Adams
2 **Ms** is used for married or unmarried women – when the marital status is unknown or if the person prefers it.	Ms C Watson
3 **Mr or Esq** is used when addressing a man. Never use both. Esq (short for Esquire) *follows* the name and is now seldom used unless an employer prefers this form. Always follow the form given in the copy.	Mr L J Henderson T Watts Esq
4 **Dr** (for Doctor) may refer to a man or woman.	Dr A T Little
5 **Messrs** is used when addressing a partnership.	Messrs Watson & Johnson
6 **No courtesy title is used:** 　*a* before the name of a limited company or a public limited company (PLC or plc). 　*b* with impersonal business names. 　*c* when a title of rank or distinction is included in a name. 　*d* with some 'professional' names.	Modown Electrical Co Ltd Marks and Spencer plc Laser Engineering Lt-Col F Rogers Sir James Winterbottom KCB Helen Kay Fashions Janet Jay, Editor

Always follow the style given in the draft copy.

● 1 **Warm-up drill**
(*figures and measurements*)

Aunt Mary's recipe for thick dark marmalade takes 1 kg of Seville oranges, 2 kg of sugar and 2 litres of water. She also has a favourite recipe for ginger marmalade which requires 1 kg Seville oranges, 1 kg apples, 3 kg sugar, 250 g preserved ginger, 20 g powdered ginger and 3 litres of water.

● 2 **Study the above information * then type the forms of address given in the right-hand column * pay special attention to punctuation and spacing.**

● 3 **Type C6 envelopes (as in Unit 48) for the following:**

　　a Mr L Holt, 24 Main Street, Eastbourne, Sussex, BN21 3EH

　　b P Goodwin Esq, 18 Lakeside Road, Ipswich, IP3 2XN

　　c Ms P Watson, 8 The Meadows, Gloucester, GL2 3BA
　　　(Mark it confidential)

　　d Regent Fashions Ltd, 14-16 Malt Lane, Wolverhampton, WV6 2PL
　　　(It is for the attention of Mr F White)

　　e Mrs J O'Brien, 13 Riverview Road, Dublin, Eire.

　　f Dr P Connolly, 79 Wembley Drive, Wembley, Middx, HA3 5SQ
　　　(Mark it urgent)

　　g Messrs Faith & Longwood, 42 Park Road, Southampton, SO2 6JB
　　　(Registered Post is to be used)

● 4 **Type the last task again, this time using DL envelopes (110 mm × 222 mm, approx 4¼″ × 8⅝″): alternatively use A4 paper folded from bottom to top into 3.**

UNIT 49　　　　Forms of address in correspondence　　　　**57**

Top headings used with marginal (side) headings may be blocked at the paragraph position *or* centred to the typing line (simple with the automatic centre function: otherwise use the backspacing method to centre each line separately).

- 1 **Warm-up drill**
  (figures)

  John has 2 homes, a town house and a country cottage. His telephone numbers are 01-969 48735 and 0254 89763.

- 2 **Use A4 paper * double spacing * block or centre the top headings * correct the ringed errors.**

EXTRACT FROM MINUTES OF
GENERAL PURPOSES CTTEE MEETING] ← (single spacing)

(held on 2 May 19--)

OFFICE
PREMISES
The Committee resumed their consideration of plans to improve the office premises. They examined 3 estimates fr local firms f the partitioning of 2 large rooms + decorating the entire ground floor. It was agreed to accept the lowest estimate + proceed/ at once with the work.

FIRM'S ANNUAL
OUTING
The Sec reported on the estimates of 3 firms in Seafield + 2 in Meadowland to cater f the (firms) annual outing this year. The best offer at Seafield was £15 a head for 2 meals for a minimum number of 60. The meals wd be served in a marquee on a suitable (sight). A limited bar service cd be arranged. At Meadowland, a similar service cd be had for £12 a head. [The Cttee nevertheless (decide) to use the Seafield firm.

DRAWING OFFICE
REPRESENTATION
The Sec reported on a request by the Drawing Office to be represented on the Cttee by virtue of (there) increased numbers. This proposal was approved.

Letters

Style of layout for letters varies from firm to firm. All the examples that follow are in the fully-blocked style (every line starting at the left margin) with open punctuation (see Unit 47). This style is the most efficient to type, and is widely used. It is acceptable in typewriting examinations.

The **ringed figures** show the number of lines of space left between the different parts of the letter. (There must always be *at least* one line of space between the different parts.) Letters are typed more quickly when they follow a consistent format (layout).

Well-typed letters are important to the image of any business. Therefore take special care with your typing of letters.

Date All letters *must* be dated. Use the date of typing unless you have a different instruction.

Salutation – the greeting that opens a letter – usually Dear Sir, Dear Sirs (when addressed to a business) Dear Madam, Dear Mr Jones, Dear Mrs Turner, etc.

Inside name and address – records to whom and where the letter is being sent. It ensures that letters are inserted in their correct envelopes, and that the carbon copies are filed correctly. Use the same guidelines as for typing envelopes – the envelope is copied directly from the inside name and address.

```
12 January 19--
  ②
Mr T Watkins
64 Old Park Road
CATERHAM
Surrey  CR3 6LH
  ②
Dear Sir
  ①
Thank you for your letter informing us that you wish to
sell your house.
  ①
Property in the Old Park district is not easy to sell
because of the proposed new motorway.  However, if the
price is right, a buyer can usually be found as there
is a shortage of houses for sale in the Caterham area.
  ①
Mr Forbes, valuer for your area, plans to call next
Saturday morning at 11 am.  Please let us know if this
is not convenient.
  ①
Yours faithfully
```

Body of the letter –is divided into paragraphs, usually in single spacing. (1½ or double spacing is sometimes used for very short letters.)

Complimentary close follows the body of the letter. Yours faithfully or Yours truly usually follows the more formal Dear Sir(s). Yours sincerely usually follows Dear Mr Brown, Dear Mrs Jones, etc.

- 1 **Warm-up drill**
  (*whole alphabet*)

  Although quite dazed and shaken, David Young fought on to win the junior boxing championship.

- 2 **Type the above letter on plain A5 portrait paper * side margins ¾″ and ½″ * top margin 1½″.**

Marginal (side) headings

Setting the machine	Set a tab stop where the marginal headings will start (5 pica, 6 elite is widely used for A4 paper). Allow at least 2 clear character spaces between the longest line in the headings and the start of the paragraphs. Set the left margin at this point, also a tab stop. Use a right-hand margin of ½″ (77 pica, 94 elite).
Marginal headings	Long marginal headings are divided – to prevent the typing line of the paragraphs from becoming too short. Start typing the paragraph on the same line as the first part of a divided heading. Marginal headings may be typed in closed capitals, with initial capitals, or in bold type. Underlining is optional. (Follow the style given in the copy.)
Typing lines with headings alongside	Use the margin release key to move back to the left edge of the paper. Use the tabulator to move to the starting position for typing the marginal heading. Use the tabulator a second time to move to the starting position (the left margin setting) for typing the paragraph.
Indent function	The above procedure is simplified if your machine has an indent function. Use it to indent the paragraphs of text from the left margin (this time where the headings begin).

Pica type and A4 paper

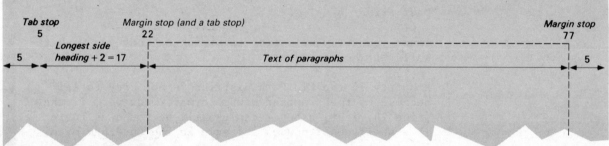

Elite type and A4 paper

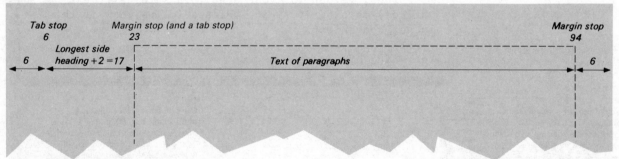

- **1 Warm-up drill**
  (shift keys)

  aA bB cC dD eE fF gG hH iI jJ kK lL mM nN oO pP qQ rR sS tT
  uU vV wW xX yY zZ aA bB cC dD eE fF gG hH iI jJ kK lL mM nN

- **2 Carefully read the above text on marginal headings * then use A4 paper to type it, following the guidelines given * top margin 2″.**

- **3 Type the text on marginal headings again, this time using double spacing.**

Reference(s) are used to file and trace correspondence. A reference often consists of the initials of the dictator and of the typist (sometimes in small letters). It may also show the department and/or a file number. The different parts are separated by a full stop or oblique stroke.

The reference on the incoming letter should be included in the letter of reply against Your ref. Where Our ref and Your ref are printed on the letterhead, align the base of the print and the type, and start typing the two references at the same point, as shown below.

Letterhead Business firms use paper with their name and address and other particulars printed at the top. A5 and A4 letterheads are included inside the back cover.

These may be photocopied for practice typing of the letters given in Universal Typing. Align your left margin to the print.

Universal Trading Group

Universal House
24 South Street
London E15 3SJ

Tel 01-474 8960

Telex 706438

②

Our ref   TLW.PT
Your ref   GKR.mp

②

27 October 19--

②

Messrs Webb & Wainwright
20/22 Hill View Road
ILFORD
Essex   IG2 4BA

②

Dear Sirs

①

Thank you for your letter of 18 October requesting 5 instruction leaflets for our Radio, Serial No MPG 112. In fact these were despatched 3 days ago, following your telephone call. We trust they have now reached you.

①

Yours faithfully

- 1 **Warm-up drill**
     (*figures*)

  Please note that we have moved from 24-26 Main Street to 157 Castle Road. Our new telephone number is 0348 9781.

- 2 **Type the above letter on an A5 letterhead.**

- 3 **Type again the letter in unit 50 * use an A5 letterhead * take one carbon copy * use today's date and Our ref JKB/ML.**

Decimal numbering system

> 1 **Decimal numbering** is a widely used modern system of numbering sections and sub-sections in lengthy reports, etc. It is illustrated below.
> 2 The main sections or items are numbered 1 2 3 etc.
> 3 Sub-sections are numbered 1.1   1.2   1.3 etc.
> 4 Further subdivisions are numbered 1.1.1   1.1.2   1.1.3 etc.
> 5 The full stop is always used to separate the figures – but there is usually no full stop after the final figure (consistently within a document).
> 6 Leave two spaces between the numbering and the start of the text.
> 7 Note the method of indenting sub-sections and further sub-sections. Each set of numbers begins at the tab position set for the previous text.

- 1 **Warm-up drill**
  (*shift keys*)

  aA bB cC dD eE fF gG hH iI jJ kK lL mM nN oO pP qQ rR sS tT
  uU vV wW xX yY zZ aA bB cC dD eE fF gG hH iI jJ kK lL mM nN

- 2 **Use A4 paper and the above guidelines.**

C A L E D O N I A N   F L O O R I N G S   L T D

EXPORT PROMOTION STUDY

Table of Contents

(Handwritten annotations: "A" above GENERAL; "6" beside European Market; "Initial Caps" pointing to WAGE DIFFERENTIALS; "4.2.3 Bonuses 30" inserted.)

Universal Trading Group   Universal House   Tel   01-474 8960
24 South Street
London E15 3SJ   Telex   706438

Our ref   ELJ/BD/1063
Your ref

②

(Date)

②

Mrs B Winterbottom
2 East Avenue
ROCHESTER
Kent   ME2 4PX

②

Dear Madam

①

I have heard from your former Branch which has refunded
the sum of £28.70 in respect of commission charged in
error.

①

I enclose a Proposal Form for Property Bond Investment,
as you requested.

①

Yours faithfully

⑤

E Jameson
Manager

②

enc

Name of sender is often typed under
the signature space. Women may
choose to have Mrs, Miss or Ms typed
either before their name or in brackets
after their name – Mrs E Smith or E
Smith (Mrs)
Official position of sender, if included,
is typed on the line following the typed
name, or it may be typed on its own.

Enclosure(s) The text of a letter usually
says something is being enclosed, but
this is not enough. As a reminder to
insert the enclosure(s) enc or encs is
typed at the bottom of the letter.
Sometimes the number or nature of
the enclosure(s) is stated (encs 2. enc
invoice, etc).
Where there is no name or official
position of the sender, leave 6 lines of
space after the complimentary close
before typing enc, etc.

- 1   **Warm-up drill**
  (*double letters*)

  Penny Hill made every effort possible to attend the
  committee meeting but arrived too late to supply the
  necessary proof.

- 2   **Type the above letter on an A5 letterhead.**

- 3   **Type again the letter in Unit 51 * add a final sentence as follows:**
  However, we are enclosing 5 additional copies * **add the name of the sender, T L Wright, and his
  official position. Assistant Manager * remember to indicate the enclosures * one carbon
  copy.**

directories[1]. It wd, however, be neither practical nor economic for BT to supply directories covering a very/wide area.

To ensure that access to all subscribers is readily available, national directory records are kept at special Directory/Enquiry Centres[2] where callers can telephone for information. The Centres are staffed by operators who provide a valuable service, but rising costs require that the calls on them are kept to a minimum. An entry in the directory therefore can help to reduce costs. [BT recognises that there are circumstances where ~~a few~~ some customers, for various reasons, are unwilling to hv their name published in the telephone directory. For these cases special facilities are available through the Enquiry Centres to ~~assist the customers in~~ dealing w callers in search of numbers that are not in the directory. The facilities are:

CATEGORY 1 : EX- DIRECTORY / NO CONNECTIONS (XD/NC)

use this style
for all 3
shoulder headings

This is a facility for people (usually in the public eye) anxious to maintain strict privacy at home. No entry relating to the customer appears in the tel directory & operators are instructed neither to connect nor report calls.

CATEGORY 2 : EX- DIRECTORY / Calls Offered (XD/CO)

This facility is f people seeking a lesser degree of privacy.

In this way the customer restricts calls exclusively to those people he chooses to make aware of his number. (Exceptionally, in cases of emergency, calls from the Police wl be offered to the customer by the BT operator.)

No entry appears in the tel directory but operators are instructed to explain to callers that the subscriber has given instructions for calls not to be connected.

Only if the caller insists on being connected wl the operator offer the call to the customer, giving him the caller's name. The customer can then ~~XX~~ decide whether or not to accept the call. As this call-filtering service makes considerable ~~demands on the use of~~ the telephone operator, a charge is made for it.

Category 3 : Callers to be connected at their request

In this case the subscriber is not seeking to conceal his telephone number but for some reason does not want any personal particulars to be published. There is therefore no entry in the directory. But the number is given by the local Directory/Enquiry Centre to any callers who enquire for it, without consulting the subscriber.

[The importance of correct directory information cannot be over-emphasized: there is nothing more frustrating for a wd-be caller than to know that a person is on the tel & he cannot get to know the number. (The caller must of course be able to provide the name and address.)

[MAKE SURE THAT BT HAS CORRECT INSTRUCTIONS FOR YOUR DIRECTORY INFORMATION.

1 The General Directory & the Yellow Pages Directory of classified ~~trades~~ trades, professions, hotels, schools, etc.

2 The number to dial is given at the front of the General Directory under British Telecom Services (Directory Enquiries).

Single Spacing

Universal Trading Group   Universal House   Tel 01-474 8960
                               24 South Street
                               London E15 3SJ   Telex 706438

Our ref   DPS/BO
Your ref

②

(Date)

②

Mr L Bruce
48 Drake Gardens
OXFORD
OX3 4BT

②

Dear Sir
①
HOLIDAY IN NEW ENGLAND
①
Further to our telephone conversation, I have pleasure
in enclosing an information brochure on the New England
States. Also enclosed is a booking form for the flights
provisionally reserved for you to travel from London to
New York on 20 August, returning 29 September.
①
Yours faithfully
UNIVERSAL TRAVEL CO

⑤

D Sharp
Assistant Manager

②

encs

Subject heading is often included in business letters after the salutation to help identify the content rapidly. This is useful when trying to find a particular letter in a correspondence file.
Typed in capital letters, with initial capitals and underlined, or in bold type.

Name of firm sending the letter Some businesses have this typed on the line following the complimentary close, as here.

- **1   Warm-up drill**
  (*shift keys*)

  Aunt Sally and Uncle Henry have invited Clare and Betty to
  Grange Farm in May or June. In October they are going to
  France where they will visit Paris, Rouen and Deauville.

- **2   Type the above letter on an A5 letterhead.**
- **3   Type again the letter in Unit 52 * add the heading REFUND OF COMMISSION * type the name
  UNIVERSAL BUILDING SOCIETY after the complimentary close * take one carbon copy.**

Multi-page documents

Multiple-page documents require consistency of treatment in the following respects.

1 **Paper** of the same size, tint, and quality for all pages.

2 **Margins** consistent on all pages – but note the following:

   a *Top margin* on second and subsequent pages – leave one inch (6 lines of space). On a first page which contains a main heading, the top margin is usually a little deeper (say, 9 lines of space) – known as a dropped head.
   b *Bottom margin* – consistently one inch. (Make a pencil guide mark at the left margin, one inch up from the bottom of the page.)
   c *Side margins* must be consistent on all pages.

3 **Numbering pages** A first page is not usually numbered. On the second and following pages the numbers should be consistently positioned – within the top or bottom margin, and at the centre of the typing line or at the right-hand margin position. The numbers may stand alone or be enclosed in hyphens, dashes or brackets.

2 -2- - 2 - (2)

4 **Headings** If the document is divided into sections and sub-sections with headings, these (whether shoulder, paragraph or marginal headings) should be consistently styled and typed to indicate clearly the text divisions.

5 **Enumeration of sections and sub-divisions** should likewise follow a consistent code to distinguish the main sections, sub-sections, and further sub-divisions. Various combinations are possible, including the following:

Section II(3)	Section II(3)d
Section II(iii)	Section II(iii)d
Section 2(iii)	Section 2(iii)d
Section 2c	Section 2c(iv)

The *decimal numbering system* is explained in Unit 100.

• 1 **Warm-up drill**
(*spaced caps*)

B E C O N S I S T E N T W I T H I N A D O C U M E N T

• 2 **A4 paper * double spacing * throughout, type BT as British Telecom.**

WP Assignment 1 *Key-in* document (BTELECOM) for 12-pitch print-out. Centre main heading in bold and embolden first part of 3 CATEGORY sub-headings. Key-in BT each time and at the end of keying-in, use the search and replace function to replace BT with British Telecom. *Text-edit* Paragraph 2 line 6: delete 'are staffed by operators who'. Use pagination facility to see where document would automatically divide into 2 pages; if unsuitable, insert a hard page break at an acceptable point. *Proof-read* text on screen, and correct. *Print-out* one copy in 12-pitch.

TELEPHONE DIRECTORY ENQUIRIES

Speedy telephone communication depends on a ready means of reference to other telephone subscribers. It is therefore important that the directories provide a comprehensive record of tel — subscribers. To encourage customers to include their names in tel — pho directories, BT provides free of charge one standard entry for each address where a customer has a telephone. Additional information or entries in heavy type are welcomed and are published on payment of an extra charge. [Customers are provided w. their local

Special marks (FOR THE ATTENTION OF, CONFIDENTIAL, etc) call for special attention and must be given emphasis – typed in capital letters, with initial capitals and underscored, or in bold type. Typed above the inside name and address, as here, they are then copied directly on to the envelope without risk of omission.

Attention line If a letter is addressed to a business (salutation Dear Sirs) but the writer wants it to be dealt with by a particular person (and/or department) this is shown. It does not mean that the letter is personal or confidential, simply that the sender knows who best should deal with it. By addressing the letter to the firm, it will still be opened if the person mentioned is away from the office.

Some firms prefer the attention line typed between the inside name and address and the salutation. Follow the position shown in the draft copy or the house style.

(Date)
②

FOR THE ATTENTION OF MR F BROWNLOW

②

Nationwide Garage Chain Ltd
22-24 Fenton Way
SHEFFIELD
S7 9EF

②

Dear Sirs
①

You will no doubt be interested to know that a completely new edition of the MOTOR STATION MANUAL is now available. As you are probably aware, this manual has been recognized for many years as an authoritative guide for service station proprietors and executives, and for students and others contemplating a career in the motor trade.
①

The enclosed copy of a press release indicates the broad coverage of the new manual which we are sure you will find valuable in your business. If you are already familiar with this work, you will appreciate the topics that have been added in this new edition.
①

The new MOTOR STATION MANUAL, fully up-to-date in every way, is priced at £12.50 (including postage and packing). However, we should be pleased to arrange for copies to be invoiced at £12 each for a minimum of 5 copies.
①

Yours truly

⑤

A Jackson (Mrs)
Circulation Manager

②

enc

● 1 **Warm-up drill**   There is no record of cheque No 24873 for £90.11 or cheque
     (figures)   No 24898 for £55.61.

● 2 **Use an A4 letterhead for the above letter * one carbon copy.**

Word processor assignments

Word processing is an important application of typewriting skills. Accordingly, 10 WP assignments (listed below and in the Index) are included throughout the level 2 work, to help you develop self-reliance at the word processor. Since terminology varies with different systems, technical terms have been kept to a minimum.

The WP assignments are presented in ruled boxes to distinguish them from the typewriting tasks, which you will normally do first. The assignments will, of course, be used for consolidation of functions already practised during word processor instruction: they should therefore be worked in the order selected by the teacher.

Document name/number Some systems make the operator identify the document before keying-in, so a suggested document name is provided for each one. An appropriate number should be assigned for systems that require a document number.

The WP assignments are in four distinct stages:

1 **Keying-in** Good practice requires that keying-in be done from the textbook drafts and keying-in instructions – *not* from finished typescript already produced in typewriting lessons (which may in any case differ in some respects). As usual, keying errors should be corrected as soon as they are noticed.

2 **Text-editing** A time lapse has to be imagined between keying-in and text-editing, during which time the originator decides on the changes given under text-editing. Any temptation to incorporate changes at the keying-in stage must be firmly resisted – or the intended practice in WP functions will be lost.

Sometimes, to help add realism, work in groups; keying-in could be done by some students and others given the text-editing, final proofreading, and printing-out tasks (in a subsequent assignment the roles being reversed).

3 **Final proofreading of the completed task** A very high standard of proofreading is essential before print-out. You must really search the VDU for errors, particularly easily-missed ones like spacing faults, mis-spelt names, faulty dates or figures.

4 **Printing-out** is required in each WP assignment since it is demotivating if the machine is cleared without taking hard copy. The hard copy should be carefully scrutinised for any missed errors.

The 10 WP assignments are included in the following Units:

1 **Envelopes** are available in many sizes, and the size best suited to the letter and enclosures should be used. The letter, etc, is folded as few times as possible, as shown below.

2 The two most widely used sizes of envelope are **C6** (162 mm × 114 mm, approx 6⅜" × 4½") and **C5/6**, also known as **DL** (222 mm × 110 mm, approx 8⅝" × 4¼").

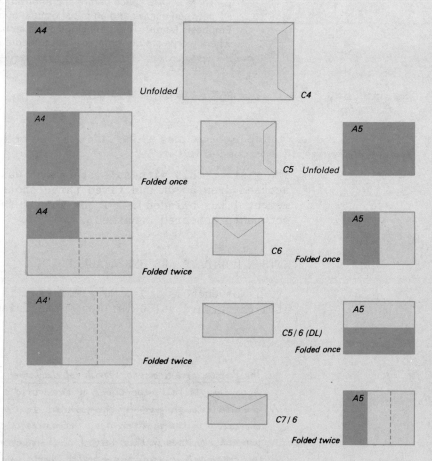

3 **Pocket envelopes** have their flap along the shorter side (as with the first two envelopes shown above). Insert them into the machine so that the flap is at the left.

4 **Banker envelopes** have their flap along the longer side (the last three envelopes shown above).

5 **Special typewriter envelopes** (banker style) are available, with a narrow rectangular sealing flap that leaves no uneven surface to be typed over – giving a better finish.

6 **Envelope qualities and tints** As with correspondence paper, a wide variety is available. Most businesses match the quality and tint of their envelopes and paper.

● 1 **Warm-up drill**
  (*whole alphabet*)

By just one reckless action in dropping a lighted match, an explosion and fire were caused which quickly razed the vast factory to the ground.

● 2 **Type a C6 envelope for your typed letter shown in Unit 51, fold the letter correctly and insert it in the envelope * type a DL envelope for the letter shown in Unit 54 (don't forget the Attention line) * fold the letter correctly and insert it in the envelope.**

Ellipsis

1 **Omission of words – ellipsis**
a Where words have been deliberately omitted from a sentence or passage (usually in quotations) this is shown by 3 spaced or unspaced (consistently within a document) full stops.
b Omitted words can occur at the beginning, in the middle, or at the end of a sentence. Sometimes whole sentences are omitted. In every case the ellipsis is shown as 3 full stops.
c There is ONE space before and after the ellipsis, but NO SPACE between ellipsis and an initial or final quotation mark.
2 **Emphasis feature** The 3 full stops can also be used in advertising copy, where words are not omitted – but to add emphasis to points.

• 1 **Warm-up drill**
   (*fractions/figures*) $\frac{1}{4}$ = 25% $\frac{1}{2}$ = 50% $\frac{3}{4}$ = 75%

• 2 **Copy twice the two following examples which illustrate the points made above: first using spaced full stops, then unspaced full stops.**

> The gist of this witness's statement was as follows. ". . . the accused drew a gun and fired three shots into the car. For a moment I was blinded . . . but when I saw the car move off the two occupants appeared unharmed . . ."

> WATSON HOLIDAYS ARE UNBEATABLE!

> . . . No vouchers . . . No gimmicks . . . No strings . . . Just straightforward value for money and friendly, helpful service.

• 3 **A4 paper * double spacing**

The Problem of a Growing World Population ← (closed caps)
According to this report one of the world's greatest problems ... is to
(✓) provide enough food ~~for the people~~. Food production has of course
increased in the modern age. Advances in science & technology have
worked wonders in this respect ... However, [due [mainly] to a welcome
improvement in medicine + health, world population has grown faster ...
There is still shortage and hunger in many countries. World population
(✓) presents a dilemma.// Epidemic diseases ~~have been~~ ^(will continue to be) brought under
greater control.[1] The average life-span is now much longer, w fewer
child deaths + adults living to a greater age. But this means more
mouths to feed... Fortunately, there is an offsetting effect in the
growing practice of ~~of~~ birth-control throughout the world. Nevertheless,
it is believed that the present world population of about 4,500 million cd
grow to 6,500 million . . . by the end of the century.[2] // On a world
scale, the scope for increased ~~agriculture~~ food production is mainly in
agriculture. More land must be made available for farming by such
means as irrigation of deserts, clearance of forests + drainage of
marshlands. Agricultural output must also be increased by more
intensive farming, greater use of fertilizers + insecticides + more
scientific plant breeding.
1 Malaria has virtually bn eliminated: deaths due to cholera +
   smallpox are greatly reduced.
2 Forecast based on recent trends + projections of birth rates
   + mortality.

Preparing letters for signature

1 Ensure that your typed letter is mailable and that the carbon copy is legible, with all corrections made on it as well.

2 Type the envelope from the inside name and address, including any special mark if there is one.

3 Clip the papers together, ready for signature:

   a Carbon copy under top copy.
   b Flap of envelope folded over the uppermost part of the top copy.
   c Secured together with a slip-on paper clip.

4 If there are enclosures, clip them together with the letter and envelope so they do not get mislaid or forgotten.

● 1 **Warm-up drill** (alphabet/comma)

a, b, c, d, e, f, g, h, i, j, k, l, m, n, o, p, q, r, s, t, u, v, w, x, y, z, a, b, c, d, e, f, g, h, i, j, k, l, m, n,

● 2 **Use an A4 letterhead * one carbon copy * type a DL envelope * prepare for signature and despatch today.**

Mr A Patel
The Limes, Langton Ave,   CHELTENHAM CH2 4BD

Dear Mr P—

(Typist – use yr initials in our ref)

SALE OF THE L——, L—— AVE

(last Wed) Following our visit to you, we enclose a copy of the particulars drawn up about yr house. You will see that we have stressed (especially) the advantages of its situation. There is no doubt that many buyers will be interested in yr house. However, to ensure (property) that we get the best offer we can quickly, we shall advertise in both the local newspapers this weekend.
// We expect a number ~~no~~ of prospective buyers wl wish to view the house on Sat & Sun & we wl telephone you to make the necy arrangements. However, if you have to go away — as you said was possible - it wd be most helpful if you cd arrange to leave a key with a neighbour: all viewers wd, of course, be escorted.
// We look forward to hearing from you.

Yours scly   J L King Office Manager
UNIVERSAL ESTATE AGENCY

● 3 **Type again the letter shown in Unit 53, adding the following final paragraph:**
I also enclose a leaflet on Venice – which you said you wish to visit next spring.
* one carbon copy * type a DL envelope and prepare for signature and despatch today.

Footnotes

1 **Footnotes** Where a document contains up to three footnotes, * ** and ***
  are acceptable footnote signs.
2 Alternatively numbers or letters (with or without enclosing brackets) are
  used throughout. Always follow the style in the draft copy.
3 The number or letter is *raised half a space in the text*, but not in the
  footnote itself.
4 In the text there is *no space* between the word concerned and the
  footnote sign. In the footnote itself there is *one space* after the footnote
  sign.
5 There must be at least one line of space between the end of the text and
  the start of the footnotes.
6 Footnotes run from margin to margin or are indented from both margins.
  They are always typed in single spacing.
7 One line of space is left between successive footnotes.

● 1 **Warm-up drill**   a1 s2 d3 f4 f5 j6 j7 k8 l9 ;0 a1 s2 d3 f4 f5 j6 j7 k8 l9 ;0
    (*figures*)

● 2 **Use A4 to best advantage for the following notice.**

AN INVITATION FROM GLOBAL PUBLISHERS[1]
80 Park Avenue, London WC2B 6AQ

Last yr we issued a general invitation to young ~~writers~~ authors to submit proposals for new books. The response was good, and two of the titles in our new GLOBAL catalogue originated in this way.[2]

Once again we shd like to hear fr ~~or~~ anyone interested in writing. We are particularly concerned with Business and Professional Studies. But we are willing to consider ~~tes~~ texts on any aspect of vocational training, or indeed any suitable matter for publication.

We shall be pleased to send a copy of our current catalogue on written request to the above address.

1 Formed by the amalgamation of Western County Publishers + the Banking Educational Press in Jan of this year.

2 ESSAYS IN ECONOMICS by J Greene, and MODERN ACCOUNTING by Ronald Black.

Display

To become an expert typist you should develop an eye and skill for **well-presented typed displays** – notices, advertisements, etc. (In display work you will need to refer to the A5 and A4 scale sheet you prepared in Unit 45.) The main points for consideration are:

1 **Skilful use of paper space** helps draw the eye of the reader to the typed material. The display should appear approximately centred on the page. Some people prefer plenty of white space all round the typed material and would therefore choose A4 paper for even short displays.

2 **Styling of lines** Thoughtful mixing of capital letters, spaced capitals, initial capitals, small letters, underlining, and bold type will help to attract the eye of the reader to key lines. (At Stage 1 level such styling will be decided by the drafter of the display for you to *copy*.)

3 **Varied line spacing** can sometimes help to emphasise key points.

4 **Layout style** Short, simple displays are usually typed in *blocked style* with every line starting at the same scale point, or in *centred style* with every line centred to the page width (shown side by side below). On manual and electric typewriters (without the automatic centring facility) the centred style is time-consuming, and therefore best avoided unless instructed. When used, the centred style *must* be accurate (centre *each* line by backspacing from the centre point of the paper, as you centred headings in Unit 32).

5 In **blocked style** the lines can begin at a guesstimated left margin position. For the best effect, however, *all lines should begin at the position that centres the longest line horizontally.* (From the centre point of the paper, backspace once for every two characters – letters and spaces – in the longest line, and set the left margin at the position reached, where *all* lines will begin.)

WOODSTOCK CHARITIES ASSOCIATION

We Invite You and Your Friends to

A   S H E R R Y   P A R T Y

on

Wednesday 6 October

1830 hrs

at

Linden, Green Park Road, Woodstock

Entrance £4.50 (including raffle)

WOODSTOCK CHARITIES ASSOCIATION

We Invite You and Your Friends to

A   S H E R R Y   P A R T Y

on

Wednesday 6 October

1830 hrs

at

Linden, Green Park Road, Woodstock

Entrance £4.50 (including raffle)

● 1 **Warm-up drill**
  (*whole alphabet*)

In his quest for a life of adventure, John met with hazards of every kind, but none more exciting than the perils of mountain-climbing.

● 2 **Use A5 paper to type the above display in blocked style * top margin 2½".**

● 3 **Type the display again on A5 paper in centred style.**

1 A **tear-off slip** usually consists of a short form at the foot of a notice, advertising, etc, to be completed and returned to an address given.

   a The tear-off slip is separated from the main material by a line of unspaced hyphens running from edge to edge of the paper or from margin to margin.

   b Leave at least one line of space above and below the tear-off line, more if there is room. If the space available is more than necessary, leave the bulk of it *above* the tear-off line.

   c The bottom margin of the paper should be approximately one inch (six lines of space).

   d Use continuous unspaced full stops or underscore for the lines to be filled in – extending them to the right-hand margin for neatness.

   e Leave one or two spaces (consistently) between the type and the start of the dotted or underscore lines.

2 **Pointers** (asterisks, dashes, etc) are sometimes used to draw attention to listed items. Leave one or two spaces (consistently) between the pointer and the start of the type.

• **1 Warm-up drill**
   (*one hand only*)

As Steve bagged a crested stag, Bert set a bear as a target.
pony pomp pupil plum plump pylon pill pump pumpkin ploy pink

• **2 A4 paper * side margins 2″ * top margin 2″ * double spacing * use hyphenation to keep an even right-hand margin * justify the continuous text if your machine has automatic justification.**

(spaced caps) → PLAN AHEAD   (centred headings)

WITH ZIRO PLANNERS

We offer a full range of planners in laminated poster form or mounted on rigid board. Supplied w planning kit of self-adhesive shapes + tapes, chart pen and ~~date marker~~ 'Today' indicator, our ~~range~~ planners wl help you to increase yr efficiency.

   * Ziro Academic Year Planner
   * Ziro Year Planner
   * Ziro Perpetual Year Planner
   * Ziro Six Month Planner
   * Ziro Staff Planner
   * Ziro 7-day Planner
   * Ziro 6 Month Holiday Planner
   * Ziro Annual Holiday Planner

Complete + return the slip below + our rep wl call + demonstrate our planners – no obligation.

- - - - - - - - - - - - -

Return to:
ZIRO PLANNERS (89) ← (single spacing)
45 Cambridge Rd
LONDON EC4 2JA

Name _____ Position _____
Organization _____
Address _____
_____ Postcode_____
Telephone No _____ ~~Ext~~ Extension ____

Vertical centring of displays can be guesstimated or calculated.

1 **Calculation method** Count the number of lines (type and space) the display will occupy from start to finish (23 lines in the display below). Subtract this figure from the number of lines down the page (50 for A5 portrait) 50 − 23 = 27. Halve the figure arrived at (13) to give an equal number of lines of space above and below the display. (Therefore *start typing* the display below on the 14th line from the top of A5 paper.)

2 **Alternative method** With paper in the machine, turn the paper back from the half-way vertical line (a lightly pencilled guide-mark) half a space (or one 'click') for each line of typing/space in the display.

Start halfway — Half a space (one 'click') for each line of typing/space

- 1 **Warm-up drill**
  (*alphabet/figures*)

He received 60 letters: there was only time to answer 45. The jar contained 123 coins - 7 of them in first-class (or even mint) condition. Did 24 or 25 come to the party? Ken ran <u>8 miles</u> in the sizzling heat!

- 2 Use A5 * blocked style, setting left margin so that the longest line is centred horizontally * guesstimate or calculate vertical placement.

<u>S U M M E R   C A T A L O G U E</u>

SEE OUR LATEST FASHIONS in

Swimsuits and Beachwear

Shirts and Pullovers

Sporty Co-ordinates

Tracksuits and Footwear

Children's Summer Fashions

* * * * * *

<u>Zenith Mail Order</u>

29 Anglesey Road
Industrial Estate
LLANDUDNO
N Wales LL3 4JK

(Tel No 0492 6843)

- 3 If you guesstimated the vertical placement of the above display, and are not happy with the result, type it again with adjustment. The only way you can learn to guesstimate satisfactorily is by scrutiny, trial and error.

- 4 Type the above display again on A5 paper * centred style * you may vary the line spacing if you wish.

Signs and symbols

1 **Subscripts** (also known as inferior or lowered characters) are typed half a space *below* the typing line, eg H_2O (water) and CO_2 (carbon dioxide). On electronics the procedure for subscripts (and superscripts) varies: check your manual. Otherwise type subscripts by using the half-spacer (one 'click'): alternatively use the interliner or variable line spacer. Subscripts are used in chemical formulae.

2 **Superscripts** (also known as superior or raised characters) are typed half a space *above* the typing line, eg $y = a^4 \times b^3$ and 30 °C. Superscripts are used in mathematical formulae and to express degrees.

On electronic typewriters some superscripts may be provided on the keyboard, eg raised 2 and 3, and the degree symbol.

3 **Mathematical signs** for subtraction and multiplication – use dash and small letter x respectively with ONE space either side. Most keyboards have keys for addition, equals, and division signs. Otherwise:
   a neatly write in the addition sign with a matching-colour pen;
   b make up the equals sign by typing two hyphens, one slightly below the other *or* neatly write in the equals sign with matching-colour pen;
   c make up the division sign by typing a hyphen through a colon sign *or* neatly write in the division sign with matching-colour pen.

4 **Dollar and cents symbols** are often provided on the keyboard. On electronics the procedure for typing 'overlay' characters varies: check your manual. Otherwise, by backspacing, type an oblique sign through capital S ($) or an oblique sign through small letter c (¢) respectively.

5 **Accents**, where not provided on the keyboard, should be neatly written in with matching-colour pen.

- 1 **Warm-up drill**
  (*shift lock*)

Let's go to the SAVOY THEATRE to see CAT ON A HOT TIN ROOF.

- 2 **Copy the following after reading through all the above notes.**

a   The chemical formula for sulphuric acid is H_2SO_4.

b $Bi(HO)_3 + 3HNO_3 = Bi(NO_3)_3 + 3H_2O$

c $y = a^2 \times b^3$

d   The following formulae are used to convert temperatures from Fahrenheit to Centigrade (Celsius) and vice versa.

    Take 5/9 of the Fahrenheit number less 32.
    Thus 77 ^oF = 5/9 x (77 - 32) = 5/9 x 45 = 25 ^oC

    Take 9/5 of the Celsius number and then add 32.
    Thus 25 ^oC = (9/5 x 25) + 32 = 45 + 32 = 77 ^oF.

e $8\frac{1}{2} + 3\frac{3}{4} - 2\frac{1}{4} = 10$

f $2\frac{1}{2} + 7\frac{3}{4} + 1\frac{1}{2} - 2\frac{1}{4} = 9\frac{1}{2}$

g $100 \div 4 = 25$

h   In New York I bought for $15.95 a suitcase measuring 2' 6" x 1' 9". This was 95¢ cheaper than the price in Dallas.

i   In the USA, the dime is a coin worth 1/10 of a dollar ($), or 10¢. A nickel is a 5¢ piece, originally made of copper and nickel.

j   The dollar sign ($) is thought to come from the Spanish dollar, or 'piece of eight' (8 reals). The S is believed to be a broken 8. The Spanish piece of eight pictured the 2 Pillars of Hercules. This may be the origin of the 2 bars that cross the S in the dollar sign in printing.

k   L'édifice est bâti moitié sur le roc, moitié sur piliers construits aux flancs du Mont Anis. L'accès principal, côté Ouest, se fait par un escalier monumental.

- 1 **Warm-up drill**
  (*whole alphabet*)

The judge thanked the witness for his lucid explanation of the events leading to the quarrel on the motor launch in Cadiz Bay.

- 2 **Use A5 portrait paper * blocked style.**

H A M P T O N   T H E A T R E

CONCERT OF FAMOUS CLASSICS

Coming Soon!

Tchaikovsky: Sleeping Beauty Waltz

Bizet: Carmen Suite

Grieg: Peer Gynt Suite

Strauss: Blue Danube Waltz

Ravel: Bolero

- and other well-loved classics

* * * * *

WATCH THIS SPACE or
Telephone 0666 4923

- 3 **Type the above display again on A5 paper * centred style * adjust the line spacing if you wish.**

- 4 **Type the above display on A4 paper * blocked style.**

- 5 **Type the above display on A4 paper * centred style.**

- 6 **Use A5 paper and either blocked or centred style for the display given below * then type again, on A4, using the style not selected for A5 * select your own line spacing each time.**

A GARDEN FETE — *spaced caps*
will be held at
Riverview Gardens, Outwood
on
Saturday 24 June at 3.30pm
in aid of
THE PARISH CHURCH RESTORATION FUND
Entrance 95p
Raffle, Sideshows, Bring-and-Buy Stall

● 1 **Warm-up drill**
(*shift keys*)

The twins' full names are Victoria Ann Carol and Gwendoline Lorna Kay. But they are always known simply as Vicky and Wendy.

● 2 **Carefully read through the following * then type with hanging paragraphs as shown.**

Hanging paragraphs are the third kind of paragraph used in typewriting, and are used far less frequently than the other two kinds (blocked and indented paragraphs).

With hanging paragraphs, the first line of each paragraph overhangs the second and subsequent lines by two spaces, as shown here. Use the indent function if your machine has it. Otherwise set the left margin where the second and subsequent lines will start since most lines will begin at that point: use the backspacer and margin release when typing the first line of a hanging paragraph.

The first-line overhang has the effect of making hanging paragraphs more distinctive, one from the other, than blocked or indented paragraphs. But they take more time and care to type.

● 3 **Copy the following, using hanging paragraphs.**

MICROWAVE COOKING

Microwaves are a form of high frequency radio (wave's). Electricity is converted into microwave energy by the magnetron tube, & is transmitted to the oven ~~capacity~~ *interior* where it is reflected, conducted, & absorbed.

Microwaves are reflected by metal so the oven interior — walls & rotating turntable — (distribute) microwaves to ensure even cooking.

Microwaves pass through but are not absorbed or reflected by some materials such as paper, glass, & plastic — which makes them ideal for cooking containers.

During heating, microwaves penetrate food to a depth of 3¾" to 1½" all round. Larger amounts of food are cooked through by conduction of heat from the *outer* /edges to the centre — and standing time is particularly important as cooking continues by conduction ~~during~~ ✓ ~~standing time~~.

Food which has bn cooked using microwave energy is not (harmfull) because ~~microw~~ microwaves are not stored but dissipated.

It was not just adventure but equally the quest for
knowledge that led explorers to face the grim hazards of
the Arctic.

● 2 **Use A4 paper * blocked style.**

THE CASTLE HOTEL ← *spaced caps*

CHICHESTER, SUSSEX

Luncheon Menu

(£12.50 including VAT)

single spacing

Tomato Soup
or
Fresh Grapefruit
* * * * *
Fried Fillet of Plaice with Tartare Sauce
Hot Roast Beef with Horseradish Sauce
Braised Liver and Onions
Cold Scotch Salmon and Salad

Roast and creamed potatoes
Fresh garden peas
Buttered carrots
* * * * *
Peach Melba
Apple Pie and Cream
Various Ice Creams
Cheese and Biscuits
* * * * *
Coffee with mints

● 3 **Type the above menu again on A5 paper * centred style.**

Roman numerals

1 **Roman numerals** are made up from 7 letters as follows: I (one) V (five) X (ten) L (fifty) C (one hundred) D (five hundred) and M (one thousand).

2 When the same numerals are repeated, they are added together: III (3) XXX (30) CC (200).

3 Where a numeral is followed by a smaller one, the smaller one is added: VI (6) XXI (21) MC (1100).

4 Where a numeral is preceded by a smaller one, the smaller one is subtracted: IV (4) XIX (19) CM (900).

5 When typed under each other, roman numerals are blocked either to the left *or* to the right (consistently within a document). Both methods are shown below.

Arabic	Capital Roman	Small Roman	Arabic	Capital Roman	Small Roman
1	I	i	20	XX	xx
2	II	ii	30	XXX	xxx
3	III	iii	40	XL	xl
4	IV	iv	50	L	l
5	V	v	60	LX	lx
6	VI	vi	70	LXX	lxx
7	VII	vii	80	LXXX	lxxx
8	VIII	viii	90	XC	xc
9	IX	ix	100	C	c
10	X	x	500	D	d
11	XI	xi	1000	M	m

6 **Use of roman numerals** (illustrated in 3 below)

a To number chapters, paragraphs, sections and sub-sections in various kinds of documents: also introductory or preface pages of a book (small roman).

b Sometimes to express the year (eg the year of making TV programmes, or on monuments).

c To designate monarchs, class numbers, and examination stages.

● 1 **Warm-up drill**
(*alphabet/space bar*)

a b c d e f g h i j k l m n o p q r s t u v w x y z

● 2 **Copy 5 above in *three* columns, leaving half an inch of space after the arabic and roman figures for number 11. Then copy the arabic and roman figures for 20 upwards, blocked to the right as shown.**

● 3 **Copy the following:** a I quoted Chapter V, Section II, Sub-section x of the report.

b The copyright line for the TV documentary reads (C) MCMLXXX.

c Henry VII, Charles II, Edward VIII, George VI, Elizabeth II.

● 4 **Use A5 paper.**

Jeremy Jones has ~~only~~ just published Part III (volumes vi to ix) of his HISTORY OF ENGLAND. Part III covers the Tudor period from Elizabeth I to Henry VII.

In Chapter XII there is a brilliant assessment of Henry VIII, while Chapter XVI contains a ~~shrewd~~ clever character study of Queen Elizabeth I. The Introduction to Part III of HISTORY OF ENGLAND is noteworthy. In the introductory pages, viii to xiii, the author traces the social history of the time. The religious struggles, fully dealt with in the body of the work, are also summarised with great clarity in pages xiv to xxv of the Introduction.

> Displays that combine **single key lines and continuous text** can be typed with a mixture of centred and blocked styles (the continuous text blocked). Otherwise the whole is blocked.
>
> The **blocked style** has a simplicity and attractiveness that is highly regarded and preferred by many people. It is perfectly acceptable at Level 1 so, unless your machine has an automatic centring facility, you may decide not to deviate from it. Use equal margins.

- **1 Warm-up drill**
  (*whole alphabet*)

  A path of crazy paving ran to the extreme end of the garden where a quick-running stream formed the boundary with the adjoining farmland.

- **2 Use A5 paper for the following display * centre the lines shown, otherwise block the whole.**

Paras in single spacing

BROMPTON RECREATION CENTRE
Winter Programme 19--

'Healthy Living'
COURSES FOR ALL AGES

VARIETY MORNINGS: Try yr hand at a wide variety of practical & useful skills in fun surroundings. From 1000 to 1200 hrs each weekday ~~morning~~.

KEEP FIT AFTERNOONS: Each weekday afternoon, from 1400 to 1600 hrs, we run 3 classes for different age groups (up to 25, 25-40, 40-60).

60-PLUS KEEP FIT SESSIONS: These are held 3 times a week, times dependent on numbers & availability of rooms. When other enrolments are complete, & the programmes finalized (end of Oct) we can give details.

PERSONAL PROGRAMME: Everyone attending a keep fit class wl be given a personal programme, devised in consultation w his/her supervisor.

DANCING CLASSES: Old time, ballroom & modern dancing classes are held each evening, 1900 to 2100 hrs.

Enrolments (in person only): 27-31 October

- **3 Type the above display on A4 paper * centre the lines shown, otherwise block the whole * paragraphs in double spacing * justify the complete text lines (having applied word division) if your machine has automatic justification.**

Correcting ringed errors

From now on, ringed errors in drafts for you to correct will be in both typescript and manuscript draft copy. You will be expected to correct the ringed errors automatically – without having your attention drawn to the fact that they are there.

- 1 **Warm-up drill**
  (*whole alphabet*)

  This boy is judged too lazy to do the work required in the sixth form. He must either be kept back a year or leave school.

- 2 **A4 paper * keep an even right-hand margin with word division * justify the right-margin if your machine has automatic justification.**

<del>TERMS AND</del> CONDITIONS OF SALE *Do not underscore paragraph headings*

1. DESCRIPTION: Each Lot is sold with all faults, imperfections, and errors of description and neither the Vendor nor the Auction-eer is responsible for the authentisity or genuineness of any Lot. Once the hammer have fallen, no purchase can be cancelled and no allowance canbe made.

2. BIDDING: The highest bidder shall be the Purchaser. The Auctioneer shall regulate the bidding and he/ she reserves the right to bid or refuse any bidding, and in the case of any Lot upon which there may be a reserve, to bid on behalf of the Vender.

3. PYAMENT: Purchasers shall give their names - and addresses if asked - and may be required to pay a deposit of 25p in the £ in part payment of the purchase money of any Lot. After a Lot is sold it shall be at the Purchaser's risk and the Auctioneer will not be responsible for it's safe <del>keeping</del> <del>custody</del>. ✓

4. Delivery & clearance: No Lots wl be delivered during the <del>time of</del> Sale & no transfer of Lots wl be permitted. Lots wl only be delivered by the Sale porter *after* the Sale in exchange for the Auctioneer's delivery order.

5. DISPUTES: The Auctioneer shall be sole arbitrators in any matter of dispute arising during or out of the Sale.

● 2

(Set out on plain A4 paper for duplication)

MEADS HOUSE FOR THE DISABLED AND ELDERLY * ← (spaced caps)

ARCHITECT DESIGNED INDIVIDUAL UNITS (FURNISHED)
(But residents may bring their own furniture if preferred)

EACH UNIT CONSISTS OF:

Bedsitting room 17' x 17' 6"
Fitted wardrobe + cupboard (aerial)
2 double power points + TV point
En suite WC, wash basin and shower cubicle
Central heating (minimum 65°)
Telephone
Lift to upper floors that will take a wheelchair
Emergency exit from each room to ~~external~~ fire ✓
escape

COMMUNAL LOUNGE AND DINING ROOM ON GROUND FLOOR
WITH ALL MEALS PROVIDED

(INSET) │ Mealtimes
│ Breakfast   9.00 am
│ Lunch   12.30 pm
│ Dinner   6.30 pm

TEA/COFFEE MAKING FACILITIES PROVIDED IN EACH UNIT

FEES
£150 per week, due quarterly in advance. 10% discount
on a full year's payment in advance

LAUNDRY/DRY CLEANING FACILITY[IES] AVAILABLE (with
service if required)

*MEADS HOUSE IS NOT A NURSING HOME — NO RESIDENT
MEDICALLY QUALIFIED STAFF ARE EMPLOYED, BUT A
WARDEN IS IN ATTENDANCE AT ALL TIMES

(Type on A4 paper)

CENTRAL ESTATE AGENCY

Selection of Properties for Sale in Newby

(Keep abbreviations)

Property	Bdrms	Price
8 Tin Lane (TH)	2	£30,000
12 Kings Road (TH)	2	£33,500
64 Hinton Road (TH)	3	£38,950
13 Mill Road (SDB)	2	£41,550
21 Fenton Road (DB)	3	£49,950
46 May Gardens (SDH)	3	£55,000
35 Oak Crescent (TH)	5	£65,750
102 Ruskin Road (DH)	6	£85,000
2 Bath Way (DB)	2	£48,000

TH = Terraced House
SDB = Semi-detached bungalow
DB = Detached bungalow
SDH = Semi-detached house
DH = Detached house

Inset 5 spaces

Production typing

There is a big difference between the speed at which one can type accurately from error-free typescript or print (copying speed) and the speed at which one can produce an accurate, well-presented document from amended draft copy (production speed).

In typing exams, production speed is of prime importance. There may also be a separate test or examination to measure copying speed: a high copying speed can, of course, assist production speed by helping to free the mind to concentrate on the needs of the task in hand. In an office, the employer is concerned solely with production speed – expecting a given document to be completed in the shortest possible time.

Production speed includes *all* the necessary processes for producing a 'mailable' or 'usable' document from start to finish. These are: preliminary reading through and noting of instructions, etc; typing the document in a well-presented manner, following all instructions, and correcting errors as they are made; final proofreading of the finished work and correction of any further errors found – or retyping *if necessary*.

To achieve the highest production speed possible, one should follow a systematic routine each time a document of series of documents is tackled. A suggested procedure follows.

1 Systematically arrange all necessary materials (typing paper, carbons, flimsy paper, envelopes, pencil, correction materials, etc) on the desk – or have them readily to hand in neatly kept desk drawers.
2 Quickly scan, read, and interpret the draft(s) for meaning and interpretation of the handwriting, drafting abbreviations, and amendments. (Use a dictionary to check unclear spellings.)
3 Highlight any special instructions regarding layout, as a reminder when typing starts.
4 Note any items that require insertion – the date on letters, enclosures, etc.
5 In the absence of specific instructions, decide the most appropriate size of paper to be used, and note whether a carbon copy is required.
6 Unless there are instructions, decide on the most suitable margins and line spacing. Insert the paper and set margins and line spacing.
7 Set tabulator stops for indenting paragraphs and insetting highlighted material, if required.
8 At the end, arrange the completed work in correct order. Assemble, with a slip-on paper clip, a typed letter, carbon copy, and typed envelope, as instructed in Unit 56.

Target times are given for the production tasks that follow. Aim to complete each document within the target time given. If unsuccessful, try to identify which activities slowed you down – and make a conscious effort to put this right next time.

All production tasks are presented as they might be given to you in an office, ie there are no printed instructions and you need to remember to insert the date and indicate enclosures, etc. Typing these documents within the target times to mailable standard will help you develop a realistic approach to office typing. Use bold type and justified right margin where appropriate.

- 1 **Warm-up drill**
  (*alphabet/space bar*)

  a b c d e f g h i j k l m n o p q r s t u v w x y z

- 2 **Carefully read through the above information on Production Typing.**

- 3 **On A4 paper, under the heading ROUTINE FOR PRODUCTION TYPING type the numbered points above.**

Task 4

Retype on A4 in double spacing, correcting ringed errors. Blocked paragraphs

COMPANY POLICY FOR HEALTH AND SAFETY AT WORK

It is the (Companys) policy that all possible steps should be taken to ensure the health and safety of its personnel. Therefore it is the duty of all (employee) to acquaint themselves fully with our Codes of Practice for Health and (Safety-and) carrying out their responsibilities as laid down therein.

All Section (Head's) must ensure that there are adequate health and safety facilities available during all production or maintenance operations. All employees with specific responsibilities for health and safety must ensure that these are adequately (delegate) in their absence.

All work procedures should be appraised periodically to (en sure) that the safest possible methods are used.

Task 5

Type on A4 paper

MELCHESTER COLLEGE OF TECHNOLOGY

Robotics — Course Number : R/12

A one-day seminar for (executives + managers) will be held on Friday - - - - - - - - (Typist - give a date of last Friday next month)

Aims
(clearer) This seminar aims to give technical + non-technical managers + executives ar understanding of the areas in which robots can be applied, + of the implications of introducing robotics into a firm.

Programme Topics

The economics of purchasing + maintaining a robot, including guidance on the ~~financial~~ economic support available.
The place of robots in manufacturing systems.
How personnel cd. be affected by the robots. introduction of
NOTE — the programme wl. include user case studies, video on robotics, discussion groups, + close w. an open forum.

Speakers
                                                    prominent
Speakers wl include users +/ manufacturers of robots.
Details of speakers wl. be issued later.
FOR FURTHER INFORMATION please complete the enclosed application form.

*Typist – carbon c+ envelope
please, for signature + despatch today*

Mr D Jenkins , 87 Tennyson Rd, Golders Green, LONDON NW11 5BX

Dear Mr J——   *Mark this CONFIDENTIAL*

We have been in touch in the past when I was working with
Consulting Partners, Johnson + Ward.
I have now set up my own executive recruitment firm + wd like to
ask yr help on an assignment I am currently handling for clients.
The position is ~~fully~~ outlined by the enclosed specification. The
client firm has been known to me personally for 3 years, during
which time I have seen them grow from a one-man start into a
well-managed + successful small company.
untapped I think it possible that they will outgrow their US parent, such
is the potential of the market ~~they are in~~ in Europe . While
the job may not be of ~~immediate~~ *personal* interest to you, I shd be
most grateful if you wd suggest any suitably qualified,
capable young sales ~~exec~~ executives who wd like the exceptional
opp—— of joining an expanding + exciting bus.
I wd much appreciate any help you may be able to give
us, + look forward to hearing from you as soon as possible.

Yrs scly
Nicola Clark

Use A5 paper

DARWIN TRAVEL

Wintersun Holidays

Spain

Portugal

Greece

Italy

Canary Isles

West Indies

* * * * *

PICK UP OUR BROCHURE
from leading travel agents

(Use A5 paper to type this form)

AXBOURNE EDUCATION AUTHORITY

Establishment . . . .

Fees Receipt No . . . .

For sum of . . . .

from . . . .

for Class No . . . .

Enrolment No . . . .

Payment by   Cheque / Cash
              (Delete item not applicable)

Signed   . . . .
              Finance Officer

Date   . . . .

b

*(Complete form with following particulars
+ today's date)*

Establishment — Alton Day Centre   [ALTON]

Rec. No   — 2407

for   — £40·50

from   — Miss G Andrews

Class No — C24A

Enrolment No — C24A/36

Payment by cheque

Typist: please retype correcting the words that are circled

A4 paper in double (or 1½) line-spacing

WHAT IS A WORD PROCESSOR?

A word processor is an automatic typewriter capable of doing a
range of operations automatically at the press of a key. It is,
in fact, a small (comptuer) dedicated to a single job.

WHAT ARE THE COMPONENTS OF A WORD PROCESSOR?

A word processor (consist) of:

Inset 10 spaces

a keyboard

a printing unit

a screen known as a VDU (Visual Display Unit)

internal memory

backing storage.

The keyboard may be attached directly to the printing unit or it
can be attached firstly to a VDU. Word processors have a small
internal memory but it is the backing storage which is (impotrant.)
Stored information is kept on diskettes or floppy disks which can
hold up to 130 pages of A4 text.

WHAT ARE THE BENEFITS OF A (WOR) PROCESSOR?

Every company requires letters and documents to conduct (it's)
affairs efficiently. The potential savings in cash and manpower
made possible by automating the paperwork are considerable. With
costs rising almost daily the benefits of greater productivity
and efficiency resulting from the use of a word (processsor) are
becoming increasingly attractive.

(RSA Stage 1)

Aim to complete the following 6 tasks to mailable standard in 2 hours.

Task 1

(Use MEMO FORM)

From / J Brown, Accounts   Ref JB/6034
      Mrs
To   Mr W Long

TRAINING PERIOD AT COVENTRY

You wl. be eligible for an allowance for each night you actually spend
at Coventry. The allowance wl. not apply if you are away from this
temp. accom. for any reason. Weekly recs. must be provided. [You can
claim for a Travel warrant every four weeks to visit yr. home. You
wl see from the enclosed claim form that you st can claim only
for visits actually made.

If you travel by train you wl. be issued w. a warrant to cover the
second class rail journey. If you wish to use yr. own car you may
claim an allowance of 25p per mile for the actual return distance between
yr. home and Coventry. [Come and see me if you have any queries.

Task 2

Our ref SS/KLM
Mrs E Winters
124 Newark Rd
NOTTINGHAM
NG9 6PQ
Dr. Mrs W—

TYPIST : CARBON COPY & ENVELOPE PLEASE

main features of the

Further to our recent telephone conversation, please find enclosed details of
our home computers together w. a comparison of the two models you
mentioned.
We can also, if required, supply a computer-compatible cassette recorder
at a price of £56.50 including VAT. A connecting lead to the computer
wd.
wl. cost around £8.75. [If I can be of any further assistance, please
do not hesitate to contact me.
Yrs. sinc.
S Shah
Computer Sales

Memos

1 **Memos** Routine written communication between persons, departments or branches within an organisation is generally by means of typewritten memos (or memorandums). Memos are simpler in layout than letters and therefore quicker to type. Their main features follow.

   a **Paper** Many organisations have their own printed memorandum forms, which vary in layout and detail. Otherwise plain A5 landscape or plain A4 paper is used. (Printed A5 and A4 memo forms are included inside the back cover for photocopying and use with the memo tasks in *Universal Typing*.)

   b A **carbon copy** is usually taken for the sender's file.

   c **Language** tends to be more informal among colleagues than in letters. The message is usually short and to the point with a subject heading, and is signed or just initialled by the sender.

   d **Delivery** is normally by hand either loose or in special heavy-duty envelopes with a name grid, usable many times. However, if the memo is marked Confidential or Personal, it should be delivered in an ordinary sealed envelope, likewise marked Confidential or Personal.

2 **Using printed memo forms**

   a Align the base of the print and the base of the type as you did when typing in letter references. Also, line up vertically the typed-in particulars as shown below.

   b Always use today's date unless instructed otherwise.

   c Enclosure(s) or Attachment(s) (att or atts) are shown below the signature space as in letters.

● 1 **Warm-up drill**
   (*figures*)

a1 s2 d3 f4 f5 j6 j7 k8 19 ;0 a1 s2 d3 f4 f5 j6 j7 k8 19 ;0

● 2 **Use an A5 printed memo form.**

MEMORANDUM

From	Miss G Whitehouse	*Ref*	GW/AD/E12
To	Mr P Allen ·	*Date*	20 September 19--

COPY FOR NEW CATALOGUES

You said you would let me have the copy for your new catalogue by today at the latest. The stock of catalogues for your Section is nearly out - see the attached list - so the matter is now <u>urgent</u>.

I have been unable to get you on the phone: they tell me you are at present working on outside business a great deal of the time. Please get in touch with me as soon as possible.

GW

att

Specimen marked task with explanatory notes

Presentation faults (5)

Two instead of three spaces between words in spaced capitals

Paragraph headings not underscored as instructed

Inconsistent spacing after colon following paragraph headings

Inconsistent line spacing after paragraphs

Transposition error – COST should appear above VENUE

Accuracy faults (9)

Month, January, not typed in full

Letter 't' wrongly inserted in 'minerals'

One word added to given text

More than one typing error in 'consortium'

Letter omitted in 'notes'

Spelling error

Capital 'B' required in first part of the postcode

Keying error – Two gs for fs in 'coffee'

Spacing error – there should be no space in front of the closing bracket

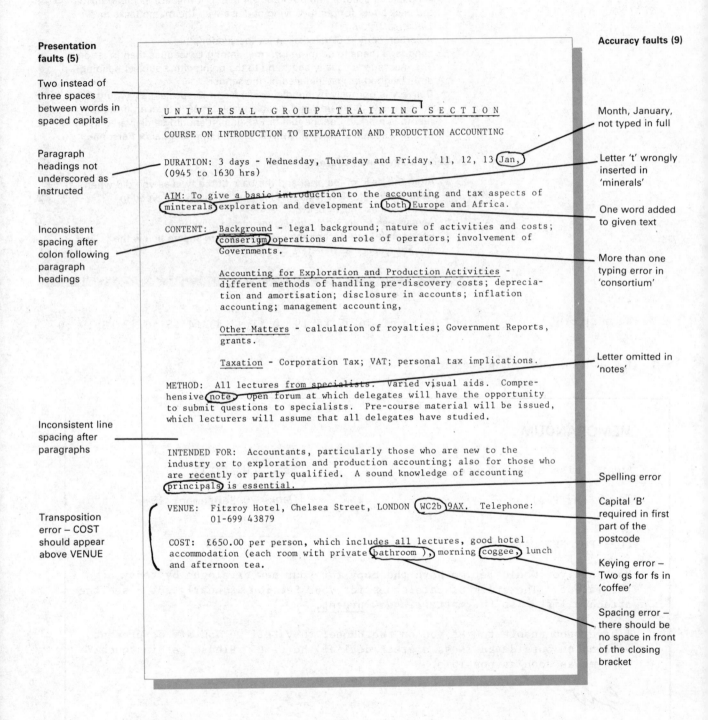

UNIVERSAL GROUP TRAINING SECTION

COURSE ON INTRODUCTION TO EXPLORATION AND PRODUCTION ACCOUNTING

DURATION: 3 days - Wednesday, Thursday and Friday, 11, 12, 13 Jan, (0945 to 1630 hrs)

AIM: To give a basic introduction to the accounting and tax aspects of minerals exploration and development in both Europe and Africa.

CONTENT: Background - legal background; nature of activities and costs; conserigm operations and role of operators; involvement of Governments.

Accounting for Exploration and Production Activities - different methods of handling pre-discovery costs; depreciation and amortisation; disclosure in accounts; inflation accounting; management accounting,

Other Matters - calculation of royalties; Government Reports, grants.

Taxation - Corporation Tax; VAT; personal tax implications.

METHOD: All lectures from specialists. Varied visual aids. Comprehensive note. Open forum at which delegates will have the opportunity to submit questions to specialists. Pre-course material will be issued, which lecturers will assume that all delegates have studied.

INTENDED FOR: Accountants, particularly those who are new to the industry or to exploration and production accounting; also for those who are recently or partly qualified. A sound knowledge of accounting principals is essential.

VENUE: Fitzroy Hotel, Chelsea Street, LONDON WC2b 9AX. Telephone: 01-699 43879

COST: £650.00 per person, which includes all lectures, good hotel accommodation (each room with private bathroom), morning coggee, lunch and afternoon tea.

- **1 Warm-up drill**
  (Shift keys)

Aunt Sally and Uncle Henry have invited Clare and Betty to Grange Farm in May or June. In October they are going to France where they will visit Paris, Rouen and Deauville.

- **2 Use an A5 printed memo form.**

From Catering Manager to All members of staff   Ref BG/SP

CLOSURE OF CANTEEN

W. effect from next Mon. the canteen will be closed for 3 wks. As you will know, the canteen is in need of ~~extensive~~ modernization ✓ & redecoration. I had ~~very much~~ hoped that all necy work wd have been carried out during last summer's 3-wk holiday break. Unfortunately, due to a last-minute misunderstanding, this was not possible. [I apologise for any incon. you may be caused but feel sure you will consider the forthcoming improvements ~~will~~ more than compensate for it.

- **3 Use an A5 printed memo form * take one carbon copy.**

To Sales Manager from Chief Accountant   Ref DW/as/12653

W CHARLSTON & SONS LTD

This firm is now considerably above its credit limit & no further orders can be accepted from them until a ~~considerable~~ (large) part of their balance is cleared.

Since you have good personal contacts with the firm, I shd. be grateful if you wd. send to them a tactful letter.

Specimen marked task with explanatory notes

letter typed on
plain paper
instead of a
letterhead

Inconsistency in
punctuation style.
Use of comma in
contrast to open
punctuation used
above

Instruction to use
closed capitals
without
underlining not
carried out

Inconsistency in
paragraph styles

No clear line of
space between
body of letter and
complimentary
close

overtyping

One word omitted

No space between
words

Spelling error

Handwritten
insertion

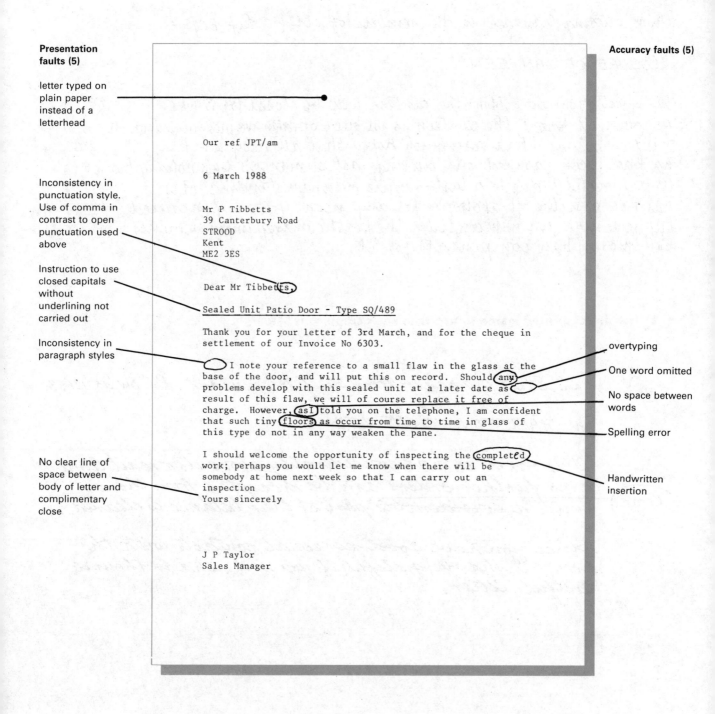

```
Our ref JPT/am


6 March 1988


Mr P Tibbetts
39 Canterbury Road
STROOD
Kent
ME2 3ES


Dear Mr Tibbetts,

Sealed Unit Patio Door - Type SQ/489

Thank you for your letter of 3rd March, and for the cheque in
settlement of our Invoice No 6303.

     I note your reference to a small flaw in the glass at the
base of the door, and will put this on record.  Should any
problems develop with this sealed unit at a later date as
result of this flaw, we will of course replace it free of
charge.  However, asI told you on the telephone, I am confident
that such tiny floors as occur from time to time in glass of
this type do not in any way weaken the pane.

I should welcome the opportunity of inspecting the completed
work; perhaps you would let me know when there will be
somebody at home next week so that I can carry out an
inspection
Yours sincerely



J P Taylor
Sales Manager
```

Plain paper memos are typed where organisations do not use printed memo forms. Layout varies – but a standard house style is usually adopted for efficiency. (Always follow the style in the copy.) A fully-blocked layout is given below.

- **1 Warm-up drill**
  (*carrier/carriage return*)

```
We
We shall
We shall send
We shall send the
We shall send the goods
We shall send the goods tomorrow.
```

- **2 Use plain A5 landscape paper.**

```
M E M O R A N D U M

From Managing Director
To    Company Secretary

AL/bc
10 April 19--

ANNUAL BOOKSELLERS EXHIBITION AND DINNER

Further to our telephone conversation earlier today, I am attaching
2 tickets for tonight's Exhibition and Dinner.  Please note that
the Exhibition will start at 1730 hrs not 1830 as mistakenly stated     hrs/
on the tickets.

I have been unable to cancel my other engagement for this evening,
and am grateful that you and a guest will attend on my behalf.

    AL

atts
```

- **3 Use plain A5 landscape paper * take one carbon copy * use your own initials as typist in the reference.**

From B G Walters to All Section Heads

Christmas Bonuses ← (caps)

It has bn decided to give/all staff the same generous Christmas bonus that they recd. last year — despite our adverse trading position at present. [Kindly inform all staff in yr Section.

paragraph – are of course taken into account.) Also penalised are: each word with an unsightly and conspicuous correction; information inserted on pre-printed forms, letterheads, and memoheads which is more than one line space above or below the related print where applicable; each instruction not carried out; work very badly positioned on the paper.

Two marked specimen tasks, with explanatory notes, are provided on pages 102 and 103.

Public examinations in Typewriting

Most examining bodies offer Typewriting or Typewriting Skills at three levels – 1 (Elementary), 2 (Intermediate), and 3 (Advanced). It is generally considered that a certificate at level 1 implies command of the keyboard, and an ability to produce a number of simple office documents accurately and with good presentation within a specified time. Successful candidates should thus be capable of general office typing at a junior level. Nearly always there is a letter, a memo, a tabulation, and a display – all from typescript/manuscript, which may be amended. A certificate at level 2 implies greater competence than at level 1, both in production speed and in the ability to tackle successfully more complex tasks: certificated candidates should therefore be capable of employment for general office typing at a higher level.

The requirements of the various examining bodies follow a general pattern in the type of tasks set, although there are some differences. It is always wise for candidates at a particular examination to be fully aware of the specific requirements of the examining body, and to have successfully (ie to mailable standard) worked through several previous examination papers within the time allowed. To this end the names, addresses and telephone numbers of various examining bodies are given below.

1 **London Chamber of Commerce and Industry (LCCI)**
Examinations Board, Marlowe House, Station Road, SIDCUP, Kent DA15 7BJ
Telephone: 01-302 0261

2 **Pitman Examinations Institute (PEI)**
Godalming, Surrey GU7 1UU
Telephone: 048 68 25321

3 **Royal Society of Arts (RSA)**
Examinations Board, John Adam Street, Adelphi, LONDON WC2N 6EZ
Telephone: 01-930 5115

4 **Scottish Vocational Education Council (SCOTVEC)**
24 Douglas Street, GLASGOW G2 7NG
Telephone: 041-248 7900

5 **Welsh Joint Education Committee (WJEC)**
Examinations Secretary, 245 Western Avenue, CARDIFF CF5 2YX
Telephone: 0222 561231

General Certificate of Secondary Education (GSCE)
This examination replaced the Certificate of Secondary Education (CSE). The syllabus is wide and varies from region to region. Full details, etc, may be obtained from the relevant authority.

a Northern Examining Association, c/o Joint Matriculation Board, Manchester, M15 6EU
Telephone: 061-273 2565
b Midland Examining Group, c/o Cambridge University Local Examinations Syndicate, 1 Hills Road, Cambridge, CB1 2EU
Telephone: Cambridge (0223) 61111
c London and East Anglian Group, c/o University of London School Examinations Board, Stewart House, 32 Russell Square, London WC1B 5DN
Telephone: 01-636 8000
d Southern Examining Group, c/o The Oxford Delegacy of Local Examinations, Ewert Place, Banbury Road, Summertown, Oxford OX2 7BZ
Telephone: Oxford (0865) 54291
e Wales, c/o Welsh Joint Education Committee, 245 Western Avenue, Cardiff, CF5 2YX
Telephone: Cardiff (0222) 561231

- 1 **Warm-up drill**
  (*figures*)

  For Account No 638791 we have no record of cheque 64502 for £248.73.

- 2 **Use printed A4 memo form.**

MEMO

From Office Manager   Ref BW/LS

To   All Office Staff

PRIVATE TELEPHONE CALLS

Our telephone bills have risen sharply during the last yr. Some of this increase is obviously due to higher telephone charges.)

But it is evident that staff are more & more using the office telephone for personal calls — instead of making use of the coin-box telephones that are provided on most floors of the building. When a member of staff uses an office telephone — & this is permissible only in an emergency — the call shd be made through the switchboard & paid for immediately. By using the ADC (Advise Duration and Charge) facility this can be done simply & accurately. I am sure you will all co-operate in this matter.

- 3 **Use plain A4 paper * use your own initials as typist in the reference.**

Typist — one cc

MEMO to Miss J Packer from J Fountain   Ref JSF/yr initials

As you know, the management of the Company have had nothing but praise for the high standard of typing throughout the Organization. But recently there have been complaints of growing delays in answering letters to the Co. In most Depts. the blame is being put squarely on the typing centre. I know you have staffing problems but wd ask you to make a special effort to speed up all typing work. If necy. I will review the limits on overtime & consider some additions to yr staff. Give this some thought & come & see me next week so we can discuss yr views & proposals.

Exam preparation

1 Know what to expect Exams are not nearly so daunting if you know what is required, and are confident that you can do it in the time given. In a class, the teacher will take care of this. If working on your own, do get a copy of your examination syllabus and several past papers (addresses and telephone numbers are provided in this Unit). Completely familiarise yourself with what is required, and work through past papers, carefully timed under examination conditions. In examinations try to use a typewriter with which you are familiar.

2 Assemble required materials Some examining bodies provide all necessary stationery, but others require you to bring your own. Check on this point. Well in advance, assemble in a folder everything you will need in the examination – practice paper for warm-up, ruler, pen, pencil, correction materials, etc.

3 Start in a relaxed mood Arrive for the examination in good time, so you can adjust your chair and arrange your work station for efficient typing. To help calm the nerves, spend a few minutes in warm-up practice.

4 Preliminary reading through When given the examination paper, check it through to confirm that the general instructions and number of tasks are what you expected from your experience of past papers. (From time to time examining bodies change their syllabus and requirements, so be vigilant.)

Quickly scan/read the paper and get familiar with the handwriting, instructions, and degree of difficulty of the tasks. Use a dictionary to check any unclear spellings. Highlight any special instructions regarding layout – as a reminder when you start to type. Note any items you need to insert – the date on letters, enclosures, etc. Some examining bodies allow five or ten minutes for all this before you can start typing. But such preliminary work is always worth the few minutes it takes.

5 Proceed from the simple to the complex If the tasks may be worked in any order, start with a simple one that you know will present no problems – to help build up your confidence. Never start with the most difficult task or you may get bogged down and flustered, and ruin your chance of success in the examination. Always ensure that you follow all instructions and use the correct size and type of paper.

6 Allocate your time efficiently In some examinations you *must* complete all the tasks to have a chance of passing. So do not rashly indulge in re-starts or immediately retype a completed document with only one or two uncorrectable errors: you may not leave yourself time to complete the paper. Do not

rush – work steadily and accurately. First-time accuracy often takes less time than relying on corrections and retyping. Wait till all required tasks are finished and proofread before you consider any retyping.

7 Assemble your papers correctly Allow a minute or two at the end of the examination to put your papers in the correct order. Draw a line through any cancelled work – or else the examiner will mark the first version that comes to hand. Assemble a letter, carbon copy, and envelope with a slip-on paper clip.

Examination assessment

In marking typewriting examinations, three components are considered: (1) speed of production; (2) accuracy of content; and (3) presentation of work. Different examining bodies apply different criteria in assessing these components: some publish details of their marking schemes, so obtain this if possible.

1 Speed of production Some examining bodies require all the set tasks to be satisfactorily completed for a Pass (eg the RSA) others allow one task unfinished or omitted provided the remaining work is good.

2 Accuracy of content Again, different examining bodies apply differing criteria of assessment. Some allocate 100 marks to the whole paper and require a certain percentage of the marks to be gained for a Pass or Distinction (eg the LCCI and PEI). Others (eg the RSA) allow only a limited number of 'word faults' overall for a Pass and Distinction.

Errors that are penalised include: each word or character string (postcode, numbers, leader dots, etc) containing typing/spelling/spacing/punctuation faults (spacing and punctuation errors counting as part of the preceding word). Usually one fault only is ascribed to any one word or character string regardless of the number of errors it contains. Each word omitted or added is also penalised, as are transpositions and misplacements.

3 Presentation faults Some examining bodies (eg the LCCI and PEI) deduct marks for presentation faults from the overall total 100 marks. Others (eg the RSA) allow only a limited number of presentation faults overall for a Pass and Distinction.

The following presentation faults are penalised: incorrect use of stationery; paper dirty or creased; inconsistency within a task of presentation of abbreviations, punctuation, paragraphing, alternative spellings, line spacing, leader dots, column arrangement, footnotes, etc. (Specific instructions to the candidates – eg an instructed change of line spacing or type of

Typing forms

You need to be able to type **forms** for duplication – to be 'filled in' by other people. Forms vary considerably in complexity. At Level 1 you will be asked to type only simple forms with simple lines. Points to observe follow:

1 Aim for good presentation on the page, with pleasing use of the space available (equal side margins, satisfactory vertical placement).
2 For legibility after the form has been filled in, use 1½ or double spacing for the insertion lines.
3 Lines should be consistently formed, using continuous full stops or an unbroken line made with the underscore key. Leave two spaces after the wording before starting to type a line.
4 Achieve a neat appearance by ending all the lines, where possible, at the same right-margin point.

● 1 **Warm-up drill**
(*whole alphabet*)

Even at the zebra crossing extreme care should be taken in crossing this wide road, as cars appear so quickly just from nowhere.

● 2 **Type the following form on A5 portrait paper. (You will fill it in in Unit 70.)**

UNIVERSAL OFFICE EQUIPMENT AND SYSTEMS

For further information on any items in this Catalogue, complete the form below and post it to:

Universal Office Equipment and Systems
Universal Trading House
24 South Street
LONDON   E15 3SJ

Please use BLOCK CAPITALS throughout.

Quote items by name <u>and</u> reference number.

Items   ....

....

Name   ....

Position held ....

Company name ....

Address ....

....

....

Telephone Number ....

Signature ....

Date ....

● 3 **Type the above form a second time – using the underscore for the completion lines. (You will fill it in in Unit 70.)**

- **1 Warm-up drill**
  (alternate hand words)

  Rated only average, my brave Polly attracted minimum credit.
  In a July bazaar in Westward Union Street, John acted loony.

- **2 Use A4 paper**

SPECIAL
∧ WINTER HOLIDAY BREAKS

From	Holiday Centre	Pages
£195	Tenerife	5-12
£190	Gran Canaria	13-16
£195	Lanzarote.	17-19
£180	Malta	20-23
£17Ø5	Majorca *	24-26
£180	Algarve *	27-33
£160	Benidorm	34-37
£155	Costa del Sol *	38-41
£210	Madeira	44-45
£195	Tunisia	42-43
£500	Barbados	46-48
£200	Rℏ Rhodes	49-50
£1²80	Athens and Tel Aviv	51-53
£180	Rome	54-55
General Information		56
Booking Conditions		57
Holiday Insurance		58
Booking Form		59

* Sailing, golf and tennis holidays are available
on special terms for parties of six or more
(see inside back cover).

- **3 Type again, each on a sheet of A4 paper, the two tables given in Unit 84 * adjust spacing if you wish.**
- **4 Type again, on A4 paper, the appointments schedule given in Unit 85.**
- **5 Type again, each on a sheet of A4 paper, the two tables given in Unit 86 * adjust spacing if you wish * use leader dots.**

Inserting typed details on forms

1 Adjust the paper so that the type, including the lower part of letters like g and p, stands *slightly* above the line. (You will need to practise this skill before you begin.)

2 Start the insertion details above the first dot or underscore character. However, where the insertion occupies more than one line (as with an address) the details may be blocked so that the second and following lines start at the same scale point as the first one.

3 Do not type an address all on one line when several lines are provided for it. Spread the parts of the address suitably over the lines available.

● 1 **Warm-up drill**
   (*whole alphabet*)

Exciting ships of every size were to be seen in the docks and in the estuary just beyond - from quaint old merchant vessels to modern liners.

● 2 **Fill in the A5 portrait form typed (with dotted lines) in Unit 69 with the following typed particulars.**

Item required : Turner Computer X 44 (Ref C 12)

Name: Edward Charles Blackman

Position: Office Manager

Co name: Southern Software Company Ltd
25 Richmond Hill
BOURNEMOUTH BH2 3ST

Tel No: 0202 73521
Use today's date

● 3 **Fill in the A5 portrait form typed (with underscore lines) in Unit 69 with the following typed particulars.**

Aztec Wordprocessor GG (Ref W27)
James Electronic Typewriter E14 (Ref T36)
Margaret Alison Rogers
Assistant Office Manager
Eagle Office Services
River Walk
Tonbridge
Kent TN9 4AD
0732 23574

Today's date please

- 1 **Warm-up drill**
  (*right little finger*)
- 2 **Use A4 paper**

Suppose I prepare a paper putting the points for the appeal?

UNISEX BOUTIQUE

A selection from our

Summer Sale Bargains

Item	Normal Price	Bargain Price
Cashmere sweaters	£85.00	£60.00
mohair tops	£50.00	£35.00
All-wool jackets	£48.00	£40.99
Silk dresses	£95.95	£80.00
Cotton dresses	£75.90	£50.00
Fine wool dresses	£80.99	£70.99
Tennis dresses	£52.50	£35.00
Top label jeans	£40.00	£30.00
Trouser suits	£76.50	£65.00
Evening dresses	£226.00	£160.00
Ski ~~trousers + tops~~ separates	£69.00	£55.00
Nightgowns	£47.50	£29.00
Pyjamas .	£51.00	£36.50

- 3 **Type again, using A4 paper, the table given in Unit 81 (PRECIOUS/SEMI-PRECIOUS STONES) * leave 5 spaces between columns * use treble spacing (two lines of space between lines of type).**
- 4 **Type again, using A4 paper, the typed table given in Unit 82 (WORDS OFTEN MIS-SPELT) * leave 5 spaces between columns * use treble spacing.**
- 5 **Type again, each on a sheet of A4 paper, the two tables given in Unit 83 * adjust spacing if you wish.**

Starting insertion lines at the same scale point With some forms the originator may prefer to start as well as end the blank lines at the same point – as shown below. (Always follow the style in the copy.)

Count the letters and spaces in the widest line of type followed by insertion lines (below – LENGTH OF SERVICE: 18 characters), allow two blank spaces, and set a tab stop (21 spaces from left margin set) to use when typing the insertion lines.

● 1 **Warm-up drill**
(*whole alphabet*)

Wise people who invested in jade and antique boxes found their money had zoomed in value. Those with money in the bank found it had lost a great deal of purchasing power.

● 2 **Type the following form on A4 paper. (You will fill it in in Unit 72.)**

U N I V E R S A L   T R A D I N G   G R O U P

PERSONNEL DEPARTMENT

Car Parking Permits

NAME IN FULL: ....

GRADE: ....

LENGTH OF SERVICE: ....

DEPARTMENT CODE: ....

I do/do not drive to work. (Please delete as applicable.)

REGULAR VEHICLE:

Make and Model   ....

Registration No   ....

Colour   ....

SECOND VEHICLE:

Make and Model   ....

Registration No   ....

Colour   ....

USUAL CAR PARK: ....

I confirm that the information given above is correct, and I will inform you of any changes to these details.

SIGNED: ....

DATE: ....

● 3 **Type the above form a second time – using the underscore for the completion lines. (You will fill it in in Unit 72.)**

Leader dots

Leader dots In some tabulations the lines in the first column vary considerably in length. In order to 'square them up', leader dots (unspaced full stops) are used. This both improves the appearance of the work and helps to lead the eye across to the related matter in the other columns.

    a Leader dots finish at the same point as the longest item in the column.
    b Leave one space before beginning the leader dots.

● 1 **Warm-up drill**
    (*left little finger*)

Zara was amazed as the squad quashed that blaze on the quay.

● 2 **A5 portrait paper * use leader dots * use space as thousand marker.**

TURNOVER IN FIRST 2 YEARS TRADING
(including departmental breakdown)

year before last ↓ | *last year*

	19--	19--
	£	£
Women's Clothing	100 879	108 964
Men's Clothing	80 750	82 000
China	35 600	40 210
Pictures	26 580	29 460
Furniture	245 760	260 233
Household	65 123	68 499
Sports Goods ...	45 163	44 281
Books	56 784	58 174
TOTAL	£656 639	£691 821

● 3 **A5 portrait paper * body of table in double spacing * use leader dots * use comma as thousand marker.**

CAWTHORNE CONFECTIONERY
Advertising Expenditure   *year before last*

Media	19--	19--	*last year*
	£	£	
National press	20,000	22,000	
Local press	8,500	10,000	
Magazines, etc	12,000	15,800	
TV..........	22,000	24,500	
Cinemas	7,600	9,000	
Hoardings	6,500	8,500	
Mail-shots	5,250	6,500	
TOTAL	£81,850	£96,800	

Deletions Where words need to be deleted on forms, type capital X through them.

● 1 **Warm-up drill**
(*double letters*)

The Finnish traveller's luggage exceeded a passenger's free allowance - but he happily accepted and paid without difficulty the excess baggage charge.

● 2 **Fill in the A4 form typed (with underscore lines) in Unit 71 with the following typed particulars. (For signature *tomorrow*)**

Susan Helen Marsh

Grade 2 Secretary

7 years 9 months

051 : 12

Drives to work, usually in a / brown Mini Metro

D538 NEL but sometimes in a silver

Honda Civic E 752 DSG. Usually parks

in George Street car park.

● 3 **Fill in the A4 form typed (with dotted lines) in Unit 71. Extract the required particulars from the following (for signature today).**

The permit is for Stephen John Williamson, a Grade 3 Engineer with 5 years 6 months service, department code 042:10. He normally drives to work in a white Ford Sierra, registration number E 486 LHC, but sometimes uses a red Ford Fiesta, reg no C 347 XXB as a second vehicle. SJW usually parks in City Road Annexe.

● 1 **Warm-up drill**
(*figures*)

All even numbers can be divided by 2 - 24, 518, 38, 198.
All numbers ending in 5 or 0 can be divided exactly by 5
- 10, 215, 45, 385.

● 2 **Use A5 paper for this appointments schedule.**

APPTS. FOR WEEK STARTING 23 MAY 19--

(Mrs G Martin)

Date	Time	Details
23	1030	Parks & Gardens Cttee Town Hall
23	1400	Planning Cttee Town Hall
24	1930	Round Table Annual Dinner
25	1100	Housing Cttee Town Hall
25	2000	Gift Day Meeting Parish Vicarage
26	1030	Friends of the Hospice St Mary's Hospice
26	1400	Finance & General Purposes Town Hall
27	1400	Tourism Cttee Town Hall
26	1830	Governors Meeting Broad Oak School

- 1 **Warm-up drill**
  (*phrases*)

  as we think, as you know, at a profit, at a loss, after all;
  as I know, as a matter of fact, at first sight, at all costs

- 2 **Use A5 paper to type the following form.**

To _____

_____

_____

Please send full information on the block
release below, which is listed in your current
prospectus.

Course title _____
Course No _____
_____

Name _____
Position _____
Firm _____
Address _____
Tel No _____
_____

Signed _____
Date _____

- 3 **Complete the above typed form with the following particulars – for signature and despatch today.**

To Westley College of Art & Technology, Westley,
London E15S 2JB

Information required on Intensive Computer
Course, No C9, by Mrs J Black, Personnel
~~Officer~~ Manager of Office Support Services, 393 Oxford
Rd, London E3J 2PQ
Tel No 01-890 78421

● **1 Warm-up drill**
(*whole alphabet*)

Fragments of black pine wax oozed over the quilt in the July sun.

● **2 A5 portrait paper.**

DAYS OF THE WEEK
(in French, no initial capital)

English	German	French
Monday	Montag	lundi
Tuesday	Dienstag	mardi
Wednesday	Mittwoch	mercredi
Thursday	Donnerstag	jeudi
Friday	Freitag	vendredi
Saturday	Sonnabend	samedi
Sunday	Sonntag	dimanche

● **3 A5 portrait paper.**

BAILEY ELECTRONICS (UK)

Midlands	North	South
Derby	Carlisle	Barnstaple
Leicester	Darlington	Chichester
Northampton	Hull	Exeter
Nottingham	Newcastle	Portsmouth
Rugby	Preston	Taunton
Wolverhampton	Sunderland	Truro
Worcester	York	Yeovil

Double (or 1½) line-spacing, on A4 paper

PRAXI LEISURE CENTRE   Typist: please retype
                                    correcting the words
Facilities Available   that are circled

The Centre has 8 squash courts, body conditioning room, boxing

room, rifle range and a main hall (fro) badminton, keep fit,

popagility, aerobics and similar pursuits. Additional (area's)

are set aside for table tennis, judo and karate. A separate

pool room and a number of meeting rooms are (avaliable) within

the Centre.

The 55-acre site also has 6 soccer pitches, 2 rugby pitches,

2 cricket pitches, a pitch and putt course, putting green,

6 netball/tennis courts and children's play area.

The (Center), with its extensive bar facilities, is also avail-

able for hire for social functions each Saturday and some

Fridays.

The tastefully-furnished Falcon Lounge Bar (provieds) a relaxing

environment for all users of the Centre, and on the outside

area immediately adjacent the game of petanque will become a

regular feature.

An extensive programme of coaching courses (are) provided for

all age groups, details of which are available on request.

Opening Hours:

Monday - Friday 10 am - 11 pm

Weekends   9 am - 9 pm

(RSA Stage 1)

Horizontal centring of tables applies the backspacing skill for centring the longest line in a blocked display (Unit 57). You will need your A5 and A4 scales sheet from Unit 45.

1 Find the longest item in each column and mark it with a pencil x. From the centre point of the paper, backspace once for each two characters and spaces in the longest item of each column, saying them to yourself in pairs as you do so. (If an odd character/space is left over from one column, carry it on to the next one.)

2 Total the spaces to be left between the columns (6 in the table below) and divide by 2. Then backspace this number of times (3).

3 Set the left margin at the scale point reached. This is where the first column and main heading(s) will start.

4 Set your tab stops for the start of columns 2 and 3 as described in Unit 81.

• 1 **Warm-up drill**
 (*whole alphabet*)

This job required extra pluck and zeal from every woman and girl.

• 2 **A5 portrait paper * either centre using the methods given *or* guesstimate placement on the paper.**

WORDS OFTEN CONFUSED AND MISUSED

affect	ensure	principal
effect	insure	principle
adverse	formally	site
averse	formerly	sight
check	lose	stationery
cheque	loose	stationary
council	past	their
counsel	passed	there
dependent	practice	whether
dependant	practise	weather

• 3 **A5 portrait paper * body of table in double spacing * either centre using the methods given *or* guesstimate placement on the paper.**

DISTANCES BY ROAD BETWEEN TOWNS

Aberdeen	Exeter	555	miles
Brighton	Manchester	236	"
Bristol	York	214	"
Cardiff	Glasgow	371	"
Dover	London	72	"
Leeds	Birmingham	109	"
Manchester	Southampton	204	"
Norwich	York	172	"
Oxford	London	56	"
London	Edinburgh	372	"

(CARBON COPY AND ENVELOPE)

Our ref HT/BW

Dr M Anderson
39 Rosewood Ave.
BROCKENHURST
Hants SO4 7ZE

Dr. Dr Anderson
15 WATERMEADOW GROVE, LEICESTER

I have today heard from the Solicitors acting for Mr
Robinson to the effect that their client is def. interested
in buying the above property from you at the ~~asking~~ price
of £39,950. This offer is made on the understanding that
~~the~~ (following) work is carried out prior to the completion date.

(INSET 5 SPACES) → WORK TO BE CARRIED OUT BY THE VENDOR BETWEEN EXCHANGE
OF CONTRACTS AND COMPLETION

1 Replace two bricks omitted from wall in roof space
   and fill in holes in chimney stack

2 Make good/ ^vertical crack approx 10¾" long in one breast in
   roof space

3 Renew back door

4 Replace four tiles on roof

7 ~~5~~ (Treat part of a purlin with Rentokil in roof space)

   ~~6~~ Remove rear eaves fascia board, liberally use
   fungicide and fit preserved piece

5 ~~7~~ (Renew lighting circuit) ←

8 Replace manhole cover by one set in grease

9 Ease or renew stopcock

10 Screw down two loose boards in rear bedroom

I will immed. proceed with the necy. Contract.

Yours sncly.
THURROCK AND LEIGH SOLICITORS

(RSA Stage 1)

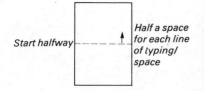

Start halfway — — — — — ↑ Half a space for each line of typing/ space

Vertical centring of tables uses the same methods as for displays.

1 **Calculation method** Count the number of lines (type and spaces) the table will occupy from start to finish (20 lines in the typed table below). Subtract this figure from the number of lines down the page, 50 for A5 portrait. (50 − 20 = 30) Halve the figure arrived at (15) to give an equal number of lines of space above and below the table. (Therefore *start typing* the table below on the 16th line from the top of the paper.)

2 **Alternative method** With paper in the machine, turn the paper back from the half-way vertical line (a lightly pencilled guide-mark) half a space (or one 'click') for each line of typing/space in the table.

● 1 **Warm-up drill**
(*alphabet/space bar*)

a b c d e f g h i j k l m n o p q r s t u v w x y z

● 2 **A5 portrait paper * centre vertically * guesstimate left margin position.**

WORDS OFTEN MIS-SPELT

accommodate	business	embarrass
achieve	cancel	essential
acknowledge	category	expense
address	colleague	foreign
apparent	committee	government
appearance	comparative	immediately
beginning	convenience	maintenance
believe	definite	necessary
bureau	efficient	parallel

● 3 **A5 paper * centre vertically * guesstimate left margin position * body of table in double spacing * take care to line up the figures correctly.**

DISTANCES BY AIR
(between airports)

London	Paris	210 miles
London	Bahrain	3,160 miles
Paris	Washington	3,830 miles
New York	Moscow	4,670 miles
Dubai	Singapore	3,630 miles
Brussels	Madrid	850 miles
Nairobi	Cairo	2,200 miles

(Use plain A4 paper)

WIMPOLE OFFICE EQUIPMENT ← (spaced caps)

HERE TODAY, HERE TOMORROW: When you buy from Wimpole, you get the extra confidence + peace of mind that only a big, well-established Co. can give you (into the bargain). We've bn around far for a long time +, above all, we value
building long-term **bus.** relationships w. you, our customers.

WIDE
~~MASSIVE~~ CHOICE AT COMPETITIVE PRICES: Look through our catalogue + see the amazing choice of office equipment we
can supply **speedily** from stock. We know you want equipment exactly suited to yr office needs, so we give you all the options you cd wish. And of course they're all of consistently ~~superb~~ **high** quality + great value for money. *

EVERY PRODUCT IS ~~INSP~~ INSPECTED + APPROVED BY EXPERTS: We expertly check, compare, + assess every office equipment product available, + select the best in each category. We still give you plenty of choice, but save you the trouble of sifting out inferior products.

LEASE RENTAL: When you're buying office equipment, it often makes gd business sense to spread the cost over several yrs by leasing it. This helps cash flow by
conserving working capital, + our arrangements w. major leasing Cos ensure you benefit from the highly competitive rates we obtain.

[CASH FLOW]

(give month)
* For the whole of next month / we are offering 15% off all cat prices.

(Leave 2" (50mm) here for an illustration)

Send to**day** for our catalogue

Wimpole Office Equipment
68-70 Liverpool Rd
BRADFORD
BD10 8XS

Blocked tabulation

1 **Tabulation** (column arrangement) assists reading and understanding of the material.
2 **Placement on paper** For best effect a tabulation, like a display, should be centred on the page (or in the space available). However, for speed you may use guesstimated top and left margins – judged according to the length and width of the table. Start by using this method – with thoughtful practice it produces acceptable results. The vital thing is accurate typing and equal space between columns. (Precise centring on the paper requires calculations, which take time. You will learn how to do this in Units 82 and 83.)
3 **Space between columns** Often the columns are all different in width. But in typed tabulation there should be equal space between columns (ie equal space after the longest item in each column). 3 spaces is widely used, and shown below.

4 **Typing method for blocked tabulation**

   a Decide and set top and left margin positions, and be ready to type.
   b Find the longest item in each column, and mark it with a pencil x.
   c Starting at the left margin set, tap the space bar once for each character in the longest item of the first column. Then tap 3 times for the blank space between column 1 and column 2.
   d Set the first tab stop here – where you will start every item in the second column.
   e Then tap the space bar once for each character in the longest item in the second column – and 3 more taps for the blank space between columns 2 and 3.
   f Set the second tab stop here – where you will start every item in the third column.

The machine is now set for typing the table, so move back to the left margin set and begin. With practice you will find the method very simple and easy to understand. The heading, like column 1, starts at the left margin set. Always complete each horizontal line in turn (using a ruler on the copy as a guide). Never work down the columns.

● **1 Warm-up drill**
   (*double letters*)

An abbey suffered a sorry fate but the killings were sadder.
Kindness and good manners really matter for a happy feeling.
The accident rate in the bigger towns in summer is horrific.

● **2   Use A5 portrait paper * follow the above guidelines.**

PRECIOUS/SEMI-PRECIOUS STONES

Alexandrite	Garnet	Opal
Amber	Jade	Ruby
Amethyst	Jasper	Sapphire
Aquamarine	Jet	Spinel
Citrine	Lapis lazuli	Topaz
Diamond	Malachite	Tourmaline
Emerald	Onyx	Turquoise

● **3   If you are not happy about the position of your typed table, retype it with adjusted top and/ or left margin. The only way you can learn to gauge satisfactory placement by the guesstimating method is by trial and error.**

Totalled money columns

1 **Money in columns with totals**

a The £ sign is placed over the farthest-left figure in the column below. Leave one line of space between the £ sign and the start of the figures.

b The decimal points must line up under each other to ensure that the tens, hundreds, thousands, etc, line up correctly under each other. (If your machine has a decimal tabulator, use it.)

c Set a tab stop for the farthest-left figure in the column. For shorter lines, tap the space bar to ensure the decimal points line up.

d There are always two figures after the decimal point even where there are no pence (12.00 in the first column below). Where there are no pounds, noughts are not required in front of the decimal point (·50 in the first column below).

e Use a comma or a space (consistently) to mark off thousands. The space method is shown below.

2 **Typing total lines**

a Do not extend the lines right or left beyond the figures in the total.

b Use the easy-to-remember 1 2 1 method (used below). After typing the last item in the column, *ensure that line spacing is at 1.* Then:

i Turn up *once* before typing the uppermost line.
ii Turn up *twice* before typing the total figures.
iii Turn up *once* before typing the first of the double lines.
iv Turn up the paper *slightly* (less than half a line space) before typing the second of the double lines.

(Use the interliner for this operation: when returned to its normal position, the typewriter automatically reverts to the original spacing. Alternatively, use the variable line spacer and manually adjust back to the original spacing.)

● 1 **Warm-up drill**
(*figures*)

a1 s2 d3 f4 f5 j6 j7 k8 19 ;0 a1 s2 d3 f4 f5 j6 j7 k8 19 ;0

● 2 **Type the money columns below. Pica: left margin 13, tab stops at 29, 45, 61**
Elite: left margin 22, tab stops at 38, 54, 70.
(Type *across* the columns, line by line, using a ruler on the copy as a guide.)

£	£	£	£
100.60	246.85	174.20	3 313.60
12.00	24.60	10.36	126.84
8.05	2.76	15.42	1 216.79
24.86	103.24	206.39	94.28
.50	3.86	69.23	2 169.67
————	————	————	————
£146.01	£381.31	£475.60	£6 921.18
════	════	════	════

● 3 **Repeat the above task until you can type it accurately and fluently.**

Statement of account

Statement of account is the document in which the seller bills the buyer for payment of goods. Statements are sent out at regular intervals (often monthly) and by a summary of all the transactions show the total amount due. Any Debit or Credit Notes are of course allowed for.
b/f means brought forward (from a previous Statement)

● 1 **Warm-up drill**
   (*whole alphabet*)

Next morning, viewing the green fields against an azure sky, we were quite decided that this was the day to join in a climbing expedition.

● 2 **Type the Statement given below.**

STATEMENT

International Book Company Limited
86–90 Kings Parade
CHESTER CH3 2BQ

To: Westons Bookshop
   16 Main Road
   LEICESTER
   LR6 4PA

Fo 96

Date: 30 April 19--

Terms: Net 30 days

Date	Ref		Debit	Credit	Balance
19--					
31 March		Balance b/f			987.50
6 April	2396	Goods	660.50		1,648.00
10 April	2486	Goods	573.50		2,221.50
12 April		Cheque		987.50	1,234.00
18 April	C 961	Returns		48.60	1,185.40
24 April	2601	Goods	550.25		1,735.65
E & O E					

● 3

Type another Statement of Account for the International Book Company Limited, using the same date. It is to their customers Aztec Book Company, 18 Castle Street, DERBY DE4 3XV

Fo 97

Typist- one cc please

Date	Ref		Debit	Credit	Balance
31 March		Balance b/f			763.50
4 April	2106	Goods	486.20		1,249.70
10 April	2487	Goods	965.60		2,215.30
18 April	2763	Goods	375.80		2,591.10
18 April	C962	Returns		51.60	2,539.50
20 April		Cheque		763.50	1,776.00
25 April	2968	Goods	254.60		2,030.60

- 1 **Warm-up drill**
  (*whole alphabet*)

At first, Hazel was extremely awkward skating on ice, but she persevered and conquered a compulsive urge just to give up.

- 2 **Use A5 portrait paper to type the following table * 2″ top margin * Pica: left margin 20, tab stop at 31 * Elite: left margin 26, tab stop at 37 * complete the second column for 8.30 am and 6.00 pm.**

<u>THE 24-HOUR CLOCK</u>

5.30 am	0530 hrs
8.30 am	
9.00 am	0900 hrs
Noon	1200 hrs
3.30 pm	1530 hrs
6.00 pm	
9.00 pm	2100 hrs

- 3 **Use A5 portrait paper to type the table below * 2″ top margin * Pica: left margin at 13, tab stop at 40 * Elite: left margin 19, tab stop at 46.**

PRINCIPAL HEIGHTS ABOVE SEA LEVEL
(in feet)

Africa: Kilimanjaro	19,340
Asia: Mount Everest	29,028
Australia: Kosciusko	7,316
Europe: Mont Blanc	15,782
New Zealand: Cook	12,349
North America: McKinley	20,320
South America: Aconcagua	22,834

Credit notes

Credit Note If any goods listed in an invoice are returned as incorrect or faulty and the seller admits liability, the buyer is sent a Credit Note showing the agreed cash difference. This is taken into account in the Statement (see Unit 80) when the buyer is billed.

Credit Notes are often printed in red to distinguish them from other documents.

● 1 **Warm-up drill**
(*figures*)

a1 s2 d3 f4 f5 j6 j7 k8 l9 ;0 a1 s2 d3 f4 f5 j6 j7 k8 l9 ;0

● 2 **Type the following Credit Note.**

CREDIT NOTE   No   961

International Book Company Limited
86–90 Kings Parade
CHESTER CH3 2BQ

To: Westons Bookshop
     16 Main Road
     LEICESTER
     LR6 4PA

Date: 18 April 19--

Reason for Credit	Quantity and Description	Unit cost	Total
Goods returned (pages missing)	3 Secretarial Practice - A Winton (Fanfare)	9.20	27.60
Goods damaged 50% reduction	4 James Burton - A Biography (Sanderson)	10.50	21.00
	Total Credited		£48.60

E & OE

● 3 **Type a second Credit Note for the International Book Company, using the same date.**

To Aztec Book Company, 18 Castle Street, Derby DE4 3XV

Credit Note No 962

Goods returned (faulty), 2 copies Dressmaking for Style - G Grace (Everest) @ £16.30 totalling £32.60

Goods damaged - 50% reduction, 4 copies Gardening for All - C Davis (Long) @ £9.50 totalling £19.00
Total credited £51.60

Invoices

1 **An invoice** is a document sent by the seller to the purchaser of goods. It shows quantity, brief description, price per unit and the total cost of the item. Each item is given a separate line, and the whole is then totalled. The layout of invoices and other business forms varies from business to business.

2 **Sample business forms** are given inside the back cover for photocopying and use with the tasks in *Universal Typing*.

3 **E & OE** (errors and omissions excepted) on business forms shows that the seller reserves the right to rectify any errors and omissions that later come to light. If the buyer has been undercharged, a Debit Note is sent by the seller: credits are shown on a Credit Note (see Unit 79).

4 **Typing invoices and other business forms** Line up the base of print with the base of type where appropriate. Set the left margin where the first column begins, and set tab stops for the start of the other columns.

- 1 **Warm-up drill**
  (*figures*)

a1 s2 d3 f4 f5 j6 j7 k8 19 ;0 a1 s2 d3 f4 f5 j6 j7 k8 19 ;0

- 2 **Using a printed invoice form, type the invoice below, following the layout given.**

INVOICE			No 2486

International Book Company Limited
86–90 Kings Parade
CHESTER CH3 2BQ

Sold to: Westons Bookshop
16 Main Road
LEICESTER
LR6 4PA

Date: 10 April 19--

Terms: Net 30 days

Quantity	Description	Unit cost	Total
20	James Burton - A Biography (Sanderson)	10.50	210.00
10	English Usage Today - B Lightfoot (Everest)	8.35	83.50
15	Secretarial Practice - A Winton (Fanfare)	9.20	138.00
20	Murder at the Inn - J Grant (Sanderson)	7.10	142.00
E & OE			573.50

- 3 **Type a second invoice for the International Book Company, using the same date as above.**

Sold to Aztec Book Company, 18 Castle Street, DERBY DE4 3XV. Invoice No 2487
50 copies of Gardening for All - C Davis (Long) @ £9.50 — £475.00
20 " International Cooking, - M Allen (Everest) @ £12.60 — £252.00
8 " Mystery of Moat Farm - P New (Sanderson) @ £9.45 — £75.60
10 " Dressmaking for Style - G Grace (Everest) @ £16.30 — £163.00
These books total £965.60

VAT (Value Added Tax) Most goods when sold are subject to VAT. Books are one of the few exceptions. Traders registered for VAT who sell taxable goods to other taxable suppliers must issue a tax invoice. This includes the seller's VAT Registration Number, the tax point (date goods supplied) and the type of supply. The VAT must be shown separately as illustrated on the invoice below.

● 1 **Warm-up drill**
   (*alphabet/comma*)

a, b, c, d, e, f, g, h, i, j, k, l, m, n, o, p, q, r, s, t, u, v, w, x, y, z, a, b, c, d, e, f, g, h, i, j, k, l, m, n,

● 2 **Using a printed VAT invoice form, type the invoice below, using today's date. When filling in the tax point column you may abbreviate the month, eg 12 Jan 88. Take care to allow for the large final total when typing the Total column.**

Invoice   No 2374

Southern Furnishings (Wholesale)

80–82 Christchurch Road

BOURNEMOUTH BH6 3DT

VAT Registration No 431 2871 63   *Date:*

Sold to: Jennings & Harlow
       86 Castle Road
       SOUTHAMPTON   SO3 4PL

Your Order No F 187   *Terms: Net one month*

Tax point	Type of supply	Description	Unit cost	Total	VAT rate	VAT amount
(date as above)	Sale	6 Armchairs No 632	85.00	510.00	15%	76.50
"	"	1 Sideboard No 248	300.00	300.00		45.00
"	"	4 Desks No 143	150.00	600.00		90.00
"	"	5 Bookcases No 325	112.00	560.00		84.00
		Total Goods		1,970.00		295.50
		Total VAT		295.50		
		Total Amount Due		£2,265.50		
E & OE						

● 3

Type another invoice from Southern Furnishings (Wholesale) to Jennings + Harlow, this time for 2 each of the same items, at the same prices, as on the above invoice. Quote Invoice No 2499 and Order No F298. Date this second invoice one month later. Fill in the amounts and totals yourself.

Blank forms

STATEMENT

International Book Company Limited
86–90 Kings Parade
CHESTER CH3 2BQ

To: Date:

Fo   Terms: Net 30 days

Date	Ref		Debit	Credit	Balance

E & OE

MEMORANDUM

From   Ref

To   Date

- -

Universal Trading Group

Universal House
24 South Street
London E15 3SJ

Tel   01-474 8960
Telex   706438

Our ref
Your ref

CREDIT NOTE

No

International Book Company Limited
86–90 Kings Parade
CHESTER CH3 2BQ

To: Date:

Reason for Credit	Quantity and Description	Unit cost	Total

E & OE

Universal Trading Group

Universal House
24 South Street
London E15 3SJ

Tel   01-474 8960

Telex   706438

Our ref

Your ref

Universal House
24 South Street
London E15 3SJ

Tel   01-474 8960

Telex   706438

Invoice

Southern Furnishings (Wholesale)

80–82 Christchurch Road

BOURNEMOUTH BH6 3DT

VAT Registration No 431 2871 63

Date:

Sold to:

Your Order No

Terms: Net one month

Tax point	Type of supply	Description	Unit cost	Total	VAT rate	VAT amount

E & OE

MEMORANDUM

From	Ref
To	Date

INVOICE

No

International Book Company Limited
86–90 Kings Parade
CHESTER CH3 2BQ

Sold to:

Date:

Terms: Net 30 days

Quantity	Description	Unit cost	Total

E & OE